OREGON, WASHINGTON, IDAHO, BRITISH COLUMBIA

Bed & Breakfast Guide

THE PACIFIC NORTHWEST

BY COURTIA WORTH, TERRY BERGER,
NAOMI BLACK, AND KATHERINE JOHNSTON

Photographs by Will Faller and
Katherine Johnston

DESIGNED AND PRODUCED BY
ROBERT R. REID AND TERRY BERGER

PRENTICE HALL TRAVEL

NEW YORK   LONDON   TORONTO   SYDNEY   TOKYO   SINGAPORE

————————————————————————————

A Robert Reid / Terry Berger production
Typeset in Bodoni Book by Monotype Composition Company,
Baltimore
Produced by Mandarin Offset, Hong Kong
Printed in Hong Kong

1 2 3 4 5 6 7 8 9 10

Library of Congress Cataloging-in-Publication Data

Johnston, Katherine.
    Bed & breakfast guide : pacific northwest / by Katherine
Johnston.
    Courtia Worth, Terry Berger.
        p.   cm.
    ISBN 0-13-068438-4 : $15.00
    1. Bed and breakfast accommodations—Northwest. Pa-
cific—Guide-books.   I. Worth, Courtia.   II. Berger, Terry.   III.
Title.   IV. Title: Bed and breakfast guide.
TX907.3.N96J64   1991
647.94795'03—dc20   91-2120
                                                              CIP

CONTENTS

OREGON

10 Mt. Ashland Inn, *Ashland*
12 Romeo Inn, *Ashland*
12 Chanticleer Bed & Breakfast Inn, *Ashland*
13 Morical, *Ashland*
14 McCully House Inn, *Jacksonville*
16 Livingston Mansion, *Jacksonville*
16 Under the Greenwood Tree, *Medford*
18 Pringle House, *Oakland*
20 Cliff Harbor Guest House, *Bandon*
22 Johnson House, *Florence*
22 McGillivray's Log Home, *Elmira*
23 Black Bart, *Junction City*
24 Ziggurat, *Yachats*
26 Ocean House, *Newport*
28 Sylvia Beach Hotel, *Newport*
32 Channel House, *Depoe Bay*
34 Madison Inn, *Corvallis*
35 Marjon, *Leaburg*
36 Mumford Manor, *Portland*
38 White House, *Portland*
40 MacMaster House, *Portland*
42 Heron Haus Bed & Breakfast Inn, *Portland*
44 The John Palmer House, *Portland*
45 William's House, *The Dalles*
46 Falcon's Crest, *Government Camp*
50 Franklin St. Station, *Astoria*
52 Franklin House, *Astoria*

WASHINGTON

56 Inn of the White Salmon, *White Salmon*
57 Haus Rohrbach Pension, *Leavenworth*
57 Brown's Farm, *Leavenworth*
58 The Manor Farm Inn, *Poulsbo*
59 Chambered Nautilus, *Seattle*
62 Salisbury House, *Seattle*
64 The Beech Tree Manor, *Seattle*
65 Roberta's, *Seattle*
66 Gaslight Inn, *Seattle*
68 Ridgeway House, *Mt. Vernon*
70 The White Swan Guest House, *Mt. Vernon*
72 The Castle B & B, *Bellingham*

74 Downey House, *La Conner*
76 Cliff House, *Freeland*
77 Channel House, *Anacortes*
77 Kangaroo House, *Eastsound, Orcas Island*
78 Turtleback Farm, *Eastsound, Orcas Island*
80 Inn at Swifts Bay, *Lopez Island*
82 Old Consulate Inn (F.W. Hastings House), *Port Townsend*
83 Lizzie's, *Port Townsend*
84 Starrett House Inn, *Port Townsend*

IDAHO

88 Hotel McCall, *McCall*
89 Knoll Hus, *St. Maries*
90 The Idaho Heritage Inn, *Boise*
92 Greenbriar Bed and Breakfast Inn, *Coeur d'Alene*
93 Gregory's McFarland House Bed and Breakfast, *Coeur d'Alene*
94 The Blackwell House, *Coeur d'Alene*

BRITISH COLUMBIA

98 The Beaconsfield, *Victoria*
98 Humboldt House, *Victoria*
100 Oak Bay Guest House, *Victoria*
101 Sunnymeade House Inn, *Victoria*
102 Abigail's Hotel, *Victoria*
104 Holland House, *Victoria*
105 Sooke Harbour House, *Sooke*
108 Hastings House, *Ganges, Salt Spring Island*
110 Old Farmhouse, *Ganges, Salt Spring Island*
112 Cliffside Inn on-the-Sea, *North Pender Island*
114 Fernhill Lodge, *Mayne Island*
115 Grove Hall Estate, *Duncan*
118 Pine Lodge Farm, *Mill Bay*
120 Yellow Point Lodge, *Ladysmith*
122 Beachside Bed and Breakfast, *West Vancouver*
124 The West End Guest House, *Vancouver*
126 Laburnum Cottage, *North Vancouver*

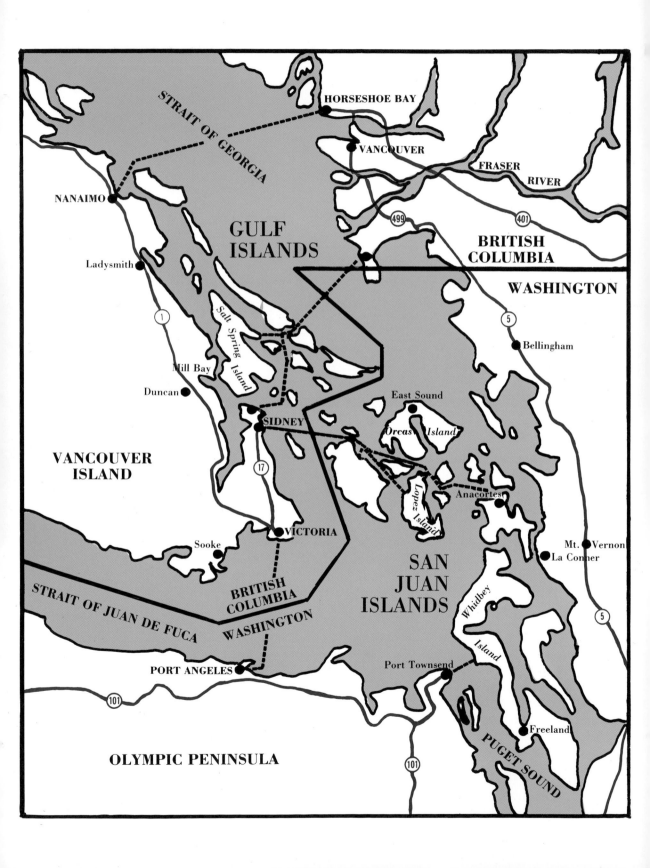

BRITISH COLUMBIA

1

WASHINGTON

Victoria

95

SPOKANE ● Coeur d'Alene

Poulsbo SEATTLE ● Leavenworth ● St. Maries 90

101 90

90

IDAHO

5

82

95

Astoria

White Salmon COLUMBIA RIVER

PORTLAND 80 The Dalles

Government Camp

Depoe Bay 80

Newport Corvalis McCall

Yachats Junction City

Elmira Leaburg 95 55

Florence

Oakland

OREGON

101

5 BOISE

80

ndon

Jacksonville Medford 95

Ashland

OVERLEAF: *Bandon Beach, Oregon, showing the ocean setting of Cliff Harbor House.*

OREGON

MT. ASHLAND INN

An awesome feat of man and nature

Poised near the summit of Mt. Ashland, the inn is an ideal place to experience the special beauty and serenity of the awesome Siskiyou Mountains while still being within easy access of the Shakespeare Festival and all the other attractions of Ashland and the Rogue Valley.

Boston transplants Jerry and Elaine Shanafelt have constructed a magnificently handcrafted bed-and-breakfast lodge from prime cedar logs cut on the surrounding land, and modeled it after places they fell in love with in the Tyrolean Alps. In rooms furnished with overstuffed furniture, Oriental rugs, and antiques amassed from their travels, they have topped-off the harmonious effect with Jerry's hand-made furniture and Elaine's handmade early American-style quilts. The guest rooms have Jerry's skillfully carved signs on their doors, with names describing the views from their windows.

The circular staircase is constructed from log ends, and doorway arches are formed from naturally-curved logs. A forty-inch stone fireplace, stained glass, and a six-foot picture window framing a view of Mt. Shasta, are all part of the wonder.

Breakfast is served at a common table, where guests may partake in the fragrant home-baked breads and a daily special, such as Normandy omelet or shrimp quiche, along with homemade granola. A "Snowstorm Special" supper, consisting of hearty soup or stew, salad, bread, beverage, and dessert is prepared in the event of bad weather, and offered to guests at a small additional fee.

Cross-country skiing begins at the doorstep, and connects by logging roads to the Pacific Crest Trail, which stretches from Canada to the Mexican border.

MT. ASHLAND INN, 550 Mt. Ashland Road, (P.O. Box 944), Ashland, OR 97520; (503) 482-8707; Elaine and Jerry Shanafelt, owners. Open all year. Two guest rooms and three suites, all with private baths, two with telephones. Rates $75 to $120 per room, including full breakfast. Children 10 and over welcome; no pets; smoking outside only; Visa/MasterCard. Recommended restaurants in area include Winchester Inn, Chateaulin, Chata. Cabaret theaters and famous Oregon Shakespeare Festival held in Ashland, and Britt Music Festival. Cross-country and downhill skiing.

DIRECTIONS: from I-5 take Mt. Ashland exit 6 and follow signs to ski area. Turn right on Mt. Ashland Rd. and go 5-1/4 miles to inn.

Left, bottom, owners Jerry and Elaine Shanafelt on the porch of their magnificent log lodge.

JOHN LAPTAD PHOTOGRAPH

MICHAEL D. DAVIS PHOTOGRAPH

The stairway is made of great chunks of cedar.

JOHN LAPTAD PHOTOGRAPHS

ROMEO INN

Poolside pleasantries

Tea time at Romeo Inn gives host and hostess Bruce and Margaret Halverson an opportunity to welcome their guests graciously. Hot hors d'oeuvres, cheese cookies, or pastry, along with great grandmother's china tea cups make this a pleasant tradition. In the cooler months, tea is served in the living room of this charming Cape Cod home. In warmer weather, guests gravitate to the beautifully secluded patio and pool. Breakfast may be served outside at poolside tables on request. Lounge chairs, a Jacuzzi, a brick barbecue grill, and a hammock strung between a couple of shady trees are so comforting that it is sometimes difficult to pry oneself away to enjoy the various theatrical performances for which Ashland is noted.

The inn, located in a residential section of Ashland, sits on the side of a hill amidst big pine trees and within walking distance of the Shakespearian Theater and downtown shops and restaurants.

ROMEO INN, 295 Idaho Street, Ashland, OR 97520; (503) 488-0884; Bruce and Margaret Halverson, hosts. Four rooms plus 2 suites, each with private bath. Two are very large with private entrances; one with fireplace. Rates: $95 to $155. Includes full breakfast of egg dish or waffles, ham or bacon. Landscaped patio with pool and spa. Central air-conditioning. No children; no pets; no smoking; Visa/MasterCard. Handicap access.

DIRECTIONS: from Siskiyou Blvd, turn west onto Sherman Street. In two blocks turn right onto Iowa, and in one block turn left onto Idaho. The inn is one block ahead on the right.

CHANTICLEER BED & BREAKFAST INN

Salmon quiche or cheese blintzes?

An exterior view of Jim and Nancy Beaver's Chanticleer Bed and Breakfast Inn reveals a simple and well-proportioned Craftsman bungalow whose strength of character derives from the softly hued porch constructed of native river stone. Entering the inn, one is captivated by its country-French interior.

The six guest bedrooms are a refreshing and sprightly mix of pastel wall coverings, coordinated floral sheets and puffy down comforters, fresh flowers, and rich carpeting. In the first-floor living room, Nancy's lustrous Haviland china collection is displayed in a glass case.

Each morning Jim and Nancy serve an especially generous and delicious breakfast in the dining room, whose windows open onto the foothills of the Cascade Mountains.

Ashland is justly famous for its high-quality Shakespeare festival, which runs year-round. Each season, the festival stages four to six Shakespeare plays as well as American classics and one original play.

CHANTICLEER BED & BREAKFAST INN, 120 Gresham Street, Ashland, OR 97520; (503) 482-1919; Jim and Nancy Beaver, hosts. Six rooms and one suite, each with private bath. Decorated in a fresh French country style. Rates: $80 to $160. Includes full breakfast with fruit course, and main entrée of baked eggs, salmon quiche, or cheese blinzes, coffee cake or croissant. Children welcome by prior arrangement; no pets; no smoking; Visa/MasterCard.

DIRECTIONS: from the south on I-5 take Siskiyou Av. exit and turn left on Third St. (just after sign for public library). Proceed ½ block on 3rd which becomes Gresham. From the north on I-5 take the first Ashland exit to Rte. 99 and turn left; 99 becomes Main St. Turn right onto Gresham just before Public Library.

to Shanghai and Yokohama. Other mementos include family photos and Pat's grandmother's oak dining room set and a rocker upholstered in needlepoint.

The grounds are elaborately landscaped. Over 10,000 square feet of lawn surrounds the house and has over 100 varieties of colorfully fragrant trees, shrubs, flowers, and rose bushes. Guests often relax on the lawn among the flowers to read or sunbathe before sightseeing and theater-going. Croquet, badminton, and putting green are extra attractions.

MORICAL HOUSE, 668 North Main Street, Ashland, OR 97520; (503) 482-2254; Pat and Peter Dahl, hosts. Five rooms, each with private bath. Rates: $65 to $95. Includes breakfast of fruits with yogurt topping, breads, and baked egg dish with vegetables and cheese, and an afternoon snack. Air-conditioned. Children over 12 are welcome; no pets; smoking outdoors. Located on Ashland's busy main thoroughfare, a 15–20 minute walk from downtown.

DIRECTIONS: from the north or south on I-5 take the Ashland Exit 19 and follow signs toward town. After the "City Limit" sign, Morical is the fourth house on the left.

MORICAL HOUSE

A masterpiece of landscaping

Turning off the highway onto Morical grounds, one glimpses the welcoming 1880s bungalow-style Victorian with its large inviting covered portico. A landscaped circular drive brings guests to the house, where the Siskiyou and Cascade Mountain Ranges hover in the background. There are sweeping views of the mountains from inside the house, especially from the carpeted sun porch where guests are enticed to linger over breakfast.

The mountains can also be enjoyed from each of the bedrooms, which are pleasantly filled with antiques, homemade quilts, and thoughtful little extras. Guests are welcome throughout the day to relax with coffee or tea in the book-filled parlor.

Family heirlooms include Oriental pieces brought back in the early 1900s when Pat's grandfather was purser on the first Pacific mail boat that went

Left, the McCully Room, which contains a portrait of Jane McCully, the original owner.

McCULLY HOUSE INN

1861 historic landmark

Jacksonville was a booming tent town basking in the glory of the Gold Rush when town physician and real estate speculator John McCully decided to build a palatial home befitting a gentleman of his stature. Soon after it was finished, however, his debts got the best of him, and he stole out of town in the dead of the night never to be heard from again. His wife Jane, being resourceful, turned the twelve room home into a boarding house, furnishing it with the finest appointments available. It was described in the 1862 local papers as "in apple-pie order and worth the price at $7 per week. . . ."

McCully House, one of six buildings original to Jacksonville, is on the National Registry of Historic Places. The Greek Revival home is graceful in its simplicity. Innkeeper Fran Wing, a design consultant for commercial interiors,

emulates the subdued elegance of the columned exterior in her treatment of the parlors and guest rooms.

Rooms are painted in soft, understated colors, providing a quiet backdrop for introducing modern touches into the historic space. Contemporary bleached-oak chairs and tables in the dining room blend smoothly with a square grand piano, original to the house, and the Victorian furnishings. A black walnut Renaissance bedroom suite, ordered by the McCully's and shipped round the horn for their new mansion, is still in place in the master bedroom.

A gourmet restaurant and café has recently set up facilities at the McCully House Inn. In keeping with the quality of the lodging, it presents a striking new dimension in upscale American cuisine.

MCCULLY HOUSE INN, 240 East California Street, P.O. Box 13, Jacksonville, OR 97530; (503) 899-1942; Patricia Groth and Phil Assetta, hosts. Three rooms, each with private bath. Rates: $65 to $75 for two. Includes a full breakfast with fruits, variety of egg dishes, breads, and fine blended coffees. In the heart of Jacksonville, 15 minutes drive from Ashland. Children are welcome; no pets; no smoking; Visa/MasterCard/American Express.

DIRECTIONS: from I-5 going north or south, take Jacksonville exit. Once in town, McCully House is clearly marked on the corner of the main street of town.

LIVINGSTON MANSION

The romance of history

Built high on a rise overlooking the foothills of the Siskiyou Mountains and the valley of the Rouge River, Livingston Mansion affords a spectacular view of Jacksonville and the surrounding terrain. From the cool depths of its western-style, paneled living room, where a fire crackles on the massive stone hearth, to the contemporary, sun-spangled swimming pool, visitors feel the romantic heritage of a historic locale.

Gold was discovered in the area in 1852, and the village attracted wealth and commerce. For a time, Jacksonville was the largest town in southern Oregon. Designated a National Historic District, today it is a monument to western history. Visitors enjoy strolling through the charming streets, where meticulously restored buildings echo the past.

Guest rooms are bright and expansive. The blue and white Amour suite has richly carved Belgian furniture and French doors leading to a charming bath with claw-footed tub and old-fashioned ring shower. The mauve and burgundy Regal suite has a fireplace, touches of paisley, and louvered doors between the rooms, making the suite suitable for families.

LIVINGSTON MANSION, 4132 Livingston Road, P.O. Box 1476, Jacksonville, OR 97530; (503) 899-7107; Wallace Lossing, owner; Bob and Elaine Srathwol, hosts. Three rooms, all with private baths. Rates: $90 and $100; November–March 10% discount. Includes full breakfast that often includes fresh fruit, muffins, quiche, herbed eggs, "Dutch Babies," and homemade jams. Business rates. No children under 12; no pets; smoking permitted outside only; Visa/MasterCard/American Express.

DIRECTIONS: from I-5 take the Medford exit and proceed west on Rte. 238. Go through Jacksonville and take a right onto North Oregon St. Continue about a mile to Livingston, take a left, and follow to the top of the hill.

UNDER THE GREENWOOD TREE

Fanciful and carefree

In Shakespeare's comedy *As You Like It*, living "Under the Greenwood Tree" refers to retreating into the forest to live in the home of shepherds and milk maids. This romantic, carefree notion describes the atmosphere of Renate Ellam's country estate. This secluded, two-story yellow farmhouse is shaded by magnificent century-old oak trees adorned with colorful hanging kites. Begging to be explored are adjacent handhewn, hand-pegged buildings dating back to 1861: a three-story cavernous old barn, granary filled with original farm tools, wagons, and plows, and a still-operating ten-ton weigh station for weighing hay wagons.

As guests explore the farm, they should acquaint themselves with *all* its residents: Henrietta, the third most beautiful donkey in Jackson County (she ate the ribbons to prove it), and Harvey, the white angora rabbit. Pigeons, partridges, pheasant, and doves are plentiful, and a pair of Bartlett finches add to the pastoral charm.

Greenwood is a gentleman's farm where luxury prevails. The décor and furnishings are first class, and no measure of comfort has been spared. A collection of crystal decanters, antique Meissen, pieces of Rosenthal china, and an heirloom wedding cup dating back four centuries exemplify Renate's fine taste. In the guest rooms, down comforters, leather bound books by Emily Dick-

A ten ton weigh station from Civil War days that still works.

inson, Lord Byron, and Robert Louis Stevenson, and perhaps an oil painting or an intricate needlepoint chair add character. The sounds of Strauss waltzes often permeate the house.

Breakfasts are abundant, with Renate's orange muffins notoriously popular. Afternoon high teas bring rave reviews, and in the evening, delectable chocolate truffles are placed on the turned-down beds.

UNDER THE GREENWOOD TREE, 3045 Bellinger Lane, Medford, OR 97501; (503) 776-0000; Renate Ellam, host. Four beautifully appointed rooms with private baths. Rates: $85 to $125. Includes full country-fresh breakfast and high tea at 4:30 P.M. Gazebo. Two miles from historic Jacksonville, the 1855 gold rush town, and 10 miles from Ashland. Children over 13 welcome; no pets although horses can be stabled (ample riding ring); smoking permitted on porches; Visa/MasterCard.

DIRECTIONS: from the south on I-5, exit 27, Barnett Road; turn left onto overpass, and turn left at first signal onto Stewart. Follow three miles until it becomes Hull. Continue on Hull one block and turn right onto Bellinger Lane.

Left, Demay Pringle, with part of her fabulous doll collection

PRINGLE HOUSE

Fantasy land for doll collectors

Sharing Pringle House with guests are several thousand others, but they don't mind the company because it gives them a chance to show off. Some are 150 years old and come from as far away as Venice, while others are brand new and as American as Shirley Temple! Demay Pringle was a professional doll dresser and restorer when suddenly, a few years ago, a client decided to sell its collection. Voila! A seed was planted and Demay's dolls now number in the thousands. The oldest belonged to a friend's great-grandmother; the tallest is papier maché and stands four feet high; the most fascinating is an Eskimo doll with red boots made from reindeer, with elaborate beading. Which one is the most loved?—well that's hard to say with so many Raggedy Anns and kewpies to choose among.

Dolls aren't all that Demay and Jim collect. China plates depicting American schoolhouses pay tribute to Jim's career as a music teacher and numerous framed prints of Scottish bagpipers displaying family tartans acknowledge a Scottish heritage. There are photographs on display of owners of this Victorian from the first owner in 1893 to the present, and in Jim's office are photographic memorabilia from his youth when he was in Hollywood's famed "Movie Choir."

Each of the rooms is filled with an abundance of Victoriana from doilies to dainty antiques, homemade quilts and thoughtful amenities. Guests are welcome to help themselves to coffee and tea throughout the day.

THE PRINGLE HOUSE, 7th and Locust Street, P.O. Box 578, Oakland, OR 97462; (503) 459-5038; Jim and Demay Pringle, hosts. Two rooms share two baths. Rates: $35 to $55. Includes a full breakfast, of fruits, daily culinary surprise, and freshly baked goods. Older children only; no pets; smoking on porches; no credit cards. One hour south of Eugene.

DIRECTIONS: from the south on I-5, take Exit 138 and proceed 1½ miles to Locust Street, the main street in town, and take a right. The house is straight ahead. From the north on I-5, take Exit 138 and proceed 1½ miles to Locust and take a left.

OREGON

Where nature restores your spirit

There is no coastline in North America that compares with Oregon's expansive beaches, roaring surf, and buffeting winds. Here nature's power is revealed in the most elemental way. You can feel its forces re-energizing you.

Respite from the elements is offered by Cliff Harbor Guest House, overlooking the spectacular rocks and surf of Bandon beach in southern Oregon. You can watch the foaming breakers, the cormorants, and the puffins from a cushioned window seat while Luciano Pavarotti's voice swells in the background from the living room stereo.

Cliff Harbor's unbelievably beautiful setting constantly renews the spirit. Guests are welcomed and can stay in two comfortably modern redwood suites. The largest has a freestanding fireplace, a full kitchen, a dressing table, two double beds, and a view of the west, where most evenings one can see the glorious colors of the setting sun sinking into the Pacific Ocean. The hospitality of the hosts allows fortunate guests to experience the exhilarating, wild beauty of the Oregon coast from a safe haven.

Bandon has several notable festivals, which include a native American salmon bake, a cranberry festival, and an old-fashioned fourth of July featuring old-time fiddlers and a fish fry.

The old section of Bandon, formerly the main part of town, is experiencing a renaissance and is now chock-a-block with restaurants, artisans, craft shops, jewelers, and a nationally recognized art gallery.

CLIFF HARBOR GUEST HOUSE, P.O. Box 769, Bandon, OR 97411; (503) 347-3956. Douglas and Katherine Haines innkeepers. Two spacious, modern suites, both with private entrances and private baths. One has wheelchair access, the other has fireplace and kitchen. Rates: $95 to $125 double. Includes a full breakfast with special egg dishes, sourdough waffles, fresh fruit and juices, chemical-free meats, and whole-grain breads. Children welcome; no pets; no smoking; no credit cards.

DIRECTIONS: provided upon reservation confirmation.

Left, sea grass covers the dunes behind the inn, which overlooks the scenic wonder of Bandon beach, above.

JOHNSON HOUSE

Turn-of-the-century charm

Built in 1892, this is known to be the oldest house in Florence. Much of its original wooden trim and detailing remain intact. Although the interior has undergone major restoration, the square symmetrical parlor and dining room have been retained.

Turn-of-the-century furnishings throughout, coupled with accents of lace, freshly cut flowers, and old sepia portraits, add to the house's charm. Included in the stay is a full breakfast of fresh fruits with cream, omelets, an assortment of breads, or Grand Marnier French toast.

Once a prosperous logging town, today Florence is a bustling summertime tourist town, with an expanse of oceanside sand dunes for wonderful beachcombing.

JOHNSON HOUSE, 216 Maple Street, P.O. Box 1892, Florence, OR 97439; (503) 997-8000; Jayne and Ronald Fraese, owners. French spoken by the Fraeses. Six rooms, two with private bath. Rates: $65 to $95. Includes a full breakfast. No children under fourteen; no pets; no smoking; Visa/MasterCard.

DIRECTIONS: from US-101, turn east onto Maple street approximately 2 blocks north of the bridge over the Siuslaw River.

McGILLIVRAY'S LOG HOME

Pancakes hot off the wood stove

For forty years Evelyn McGillivray dreamed of living in a log house. Finally that dream came true, when with vision and ingenuity plans were drawn up and an extraordinary log home was masterminded.

The bark was peeled off hundreds of huge, hand-picked Oregon fir, spruce, cedar, oak, and pine. It took two years to build this dream house where sixteen-foot beams, fourteen inches in diameter, create a setting Paul Bunyan could have considered home. The split log open staircase, the high cathedral ceiling and rustic stone wall separating the living room wood stove from the fine Langwood cooking stove, combine to make McGillivray's a very special place indeed.

Being a guest at McGillivray's is assuredly wonderful, and breakfast is amazing. Evelyn gets the fire in the stove up to perfect temperature and then, using an antique square pancake griddle, produces the best pancakes ever created. Crushed filberts blended into honey butter and a topping made with berries from the garden, almost pre-empt the warm maple syrup.

One young visitor asked his hosts with envy and disbelief, "Do you get to live here all the time?"

McGILLIVRAY'S LOG HOME, 88680 Evers Road, Elmira, OR 97437; (503) 935-3564; Evelyn McGillivray, host. Two rooms with private baths and king-sized beds. Rates: $50 to $60. Includes a lovingly prepared full breakfast and refreshments and cheese in the afternoon. Children are welcome; no pets; smoking on porches; Visa/MasterCard. Handicap access.

DIRECTIONS: from Eugene take Rte. 126 west to Elmira and turn left on Suttle Rd. for 2 miles. At Evers Rd. turn right to 5th driveway on left. look for black and white pole with log bird house on top that marks the driveway.

Frilly Victorian luxury.

BLACK BART

Gregarious innkeepers

No strangers to rural living, Irma and Don Mode moved to Junction City, just fifteen miles northwest of Eugene, and ninety minutes from the Oregon coast. Operating a bed and breakfast seemed like a good way for this gregarious couple to meet people, and become part of the community. The Modes purchased an 1880s home, and remodeled it to reveal windows formerly hidden by a wall, and to provide twentieth-century conveniences for bed and breakfast guest accommodations.

Set among stately maples and redwoods, the surrounding gardens are ablaze in seasonal blooms ranging from tulips and rhododendrons in spring, to dahlias, marigolds, and petunias in summer. Encircled by these glorious blossoms, a large country table in an add-on glass-enclosed sun room sets the scene for a hearty breakfast. Irma serves a mouth-watering combination of country and ethnic cooking, which might include homemade apple sauce, fresh country eggs, Danish pancakes (*aebleskivers*) with rhubarb syrup, or perhaps strawberry pancakes, Bohemian *Liwanzen*, muffins, and marionberry jam.

A formal front parlor is reminiscent of a by-gone age, with wainscoting, wallpaper, valanced curtains, and china-display cabinets. The guest rooms also evoke images of the past, with early-American antiques, canopied or brass beds, and ruffled Priscilla curtains. On the stairway walls is a charming vintage assortment of family photos focusing on Irma's and Don's ancestors.

BLACK BART, 94125 Love Lake Rd., Junction City, OR 97448; (503) 998-1904. Don and Irma Mode, owners. Open all year. Two rooms with king sized beds and private baths. Rates: $50 single, $60 double, including full breakfast. Children over 12; no pets; no smoking; Visa/MasterCard. Resident dog, Mischief. Irma sells original characters from the bestseller "Gnomes" and the Sandman Collection, handcrafted in Oregon. Fine dining 20 minutes away in Eugene. Scandinavian Festival in early August, golf, winery tours, cycling, jogging, swimming, boating.

DIRECTIONS: *from the north*: take exit 216 off I-5 and go west to Halsey; turn left on 99E south to Junction City; proceed to 3rd stoplight; turn left on First St.; continue approximately 1.4 miles where road curves and Love Lake Rd. joins on the left; turn left on Love Lake Rd. and Black Bart is first house on right. *From the south*: take exit 195 off I-5 and go west on Beltline Rd. for 4.1 miles; turn right at River Road and continue 8.3 miles to Love Lake Rd.; turn right and Black Bart is first house on right.

ZIGGURAT

Magnificent ocean views

About four years ago Ziggurat materialized from an exciting concept of Eugene architect Monte Marshall. Hundreds of people stopped by endlessly to observe and wonder. Mary Lou Cavendish and Irving Tebor, the owners, had no idea that their Oregon cedar-shingled house would generate such passionate interest.

The structure, a four-story pyramid, rises majestically on the Oregon coast between the Pacific Ocean and the Coast Range Mountains. Designed to be visually exciting both inside and out, the slanted windows offer insiders vignette views of memorable sunsets, Ten Mile River where steelhead and salmon spawn, and the vast ocean.

Two stylishly contemporary suites on the first floor share a commodious bath and sauna. The décor in the guest rooms, strikingly contemporary, features hand-patterned wallpapers, built-ins,

Left above, a wonder of modern architecture, with an even more wondrous ocean view. Below, a harmony of interior furnishings.

Northwest-coast art, whale prints, and Brazilian artwork. An expansive library/living room, comfortably and pleasingly furnished, is well stocked with books and games. A tiled solarium with panoramic views of the ocean completes the domain of the bed and breakfast on the first floor. For those who prefer not to view the ocean from behind glass panels, there are outdoor decks.

Another magnificent view of the ocean is seen from the second-floor dining room, where guests are served the same scrumptious breakfast their hosts enjoy. Lots of fresh fruit, Irv's homemade bread, a concoction of sautéed potatoes, onion, and pepper bacon, scrambled eggs, blueberry pancakes, or walnut waffles are popular fare. In Yachats, Indian for "where the stone turns to sand," some six miles away, La Serre, a fine restaurant, is recommended for excellent dinners.

Canada geese stop by on their migratory flights and there are blue heron, gulls, and long red-beaked oyster catchers to glimpse. Tidal pools reveal anemones, sea urchins, and starfish.

ZIGGURAT, 95330 Highway 101, P.O. Box 757, Yachats, OR 97498; (503) 547-3925; Mary Lou Cavendish and Irving Tebor, owners. Two large suites with shared commodious bath with sauna. Rates: $65 single, $75 double, $110 for entire first floor for 2 people, extra person $15 (maximum 4). Includes full and ample breakfast. Children over fourteen; no pets; no smoking; no credit cards. Close to Cape Perpetua, the dunes, the Marine Science Center, and numerous state parks.

DIRECTIONS: about 19 miles north of Florence on Hwy. 101.

PHOTOGRAPHS COURTESY ZIGGURAT

A memorable breakfast experience.

Left, Agate Beach. Above, the gardens bloom all year long.

OCEAN HOUSE

Commanding ocean views

Ocean House is certainly one of the most sensational bed and breakfast sites on the Oregon coast. Perched high above Agate Beach, it commands ocean views that bring guests back year after year. Strategically located platforms at the cliff's edge offer peaceful retreats for sipping morning coffee, or for watching the enchanting sunsets.

Adding to the location's natural charms, owners Bob and Bette Garrard have surrounded their Cape Cod-style home with glorious gardens, and tending the bounty of blooms is their special joy.

From the Ocean House garden, a private trail eases down the cliff to a secluded beach, perfect for walking, jogging, watching the surfers, and exploring tide pools. Winter storm-watching has become a popular coastal pastime, and the Garrards have added a bay window, with weather-station instruments recording barometric pressure and wind velocity. It is the perfect spot to observe nature's

forces from a safe and comfortable vantage point indoors, beside a roaring fire.

All four guest rooms have ocean views, and one features a spacious deck overlooking the garden as well. The décor of the individually styled rooms is homey and unpretentious, with emphasis on pastel shades, wicker furniture, brass headboards, lace curtains, and eyelet bedspreads.

"We raised our family here, and we didn't really want to leave when they grew up", says Bob warmly, regarding the decision to open his home to guests. "We've always enjoyed people, the yard, and the home itself, so the situation was ripe for a bed and breakfast. It worked out just perfectly, and its getting better all the time."

OCEAN HOUSE, 4920 NW Woody Way, Newport, OR 97365; (503) 265-6158/265-7779. Bob and Bette Garrard, owners. Open all year except Christmas holidays. Four rooms, all with private baths, ocean views, and one with deck. Rates: $62.50 to $94. A full breakfast is served in the spacious living room or on the sunny deck. No children; no pets; no smoking inside. Lots of good restaurants in Newport. Nearby Yaquina Head Lighthouse features a large observation deck for viewing seals and migrating grey whales, with information provided by Oregon State University volunteers.

DIRECTIONS: *from the north*: on Hwy 101 into Newport, watch for blue and white Oregon State sign 2 blocks south of Yaquina Head Lighthouse road, then turn right. *From the south*: on Hwy 101 into Newport, pass Agate Beach Golf Club, watch for Oregon State sign and turn left.

Left, the galleried library. Above, the Agatha Christie Room.

SYLVIA BEACH HOTEL

Where Agatha Christie meets Edgar Allan Poe

It would be difficult to find a bed and breakfast to equal the Sylvia Beach.

Since its beginnings, in the early 1900s, the hotel suffered through many years of changing ownership. Fortunately, current owners Sally Ford and Goody Cable, bought this cliff-side landmark in 1984, and gave the hotel a thorough facelift. Prompted by their love of arts and literature, Sally and Goody named the hotel after the owner of Shakespeare & Company Bookstore in Paris. Sylvia Beach was a long-time friend and supporter to many of the so-called "Lost Generation," a group of American and English writers of the 1920s and 1930s.

Twenty guest rooms, most with alluring ocean views, are not only named after famous (and a few lesser-known) authors, but are furnished in décor which depicts their writings and personalities. Agatha Christie fans might choose to sleep in the attractive room named for her, with ocean-front windows, deck, fireplace, and clues to 80 murder mysteries. Gauzy mosquito netting and a steamy ambience characterize the Tennessee Williams room, while the Ernest Hemingway room portrays his fascination with Africa, and the Edgar Allan Poe room is a must for those with a taste for the macabre.

On the top floor is an inviting library, with a fireplace, comfortable chairs, coffee, and tea—all that is needed to relax and enjoy the stacks of books on the mezzanine shelves. The Table of Contents dining room accommodates guests for breakfast and fixed-menu gourmet dinners, with guests seated around tables for eight. From the hotel's lofty position, forty feet above the beach, the dining room picture windows frame glorious coastal sunsets.

SYLVIA BEACH HOTEL, 267 N.W. Cliff, Newport, OR 97365; (503) 265-5428. Sally Ford and Goody Cable, owners; Ken Peyton, manager; Charlotte Dinolt, assistant manager. Open all year. Twenty guest rooms, all with private baths; 3 with oceanfront views/fireplaces/ decks; 13 with ocean views. Rates: $40 to $110 single; $50 to $120 double; some rooms with higher rates on weekends and holidays. Includes full breakfast. Children over 10 welcome; no pets; no smoking inside; Visa/MasterCard/American Express. Award winning restaurant on premises for dinner. Beachcombing, tidepools, agate hunting, clamming, scenic drives in the area.

DIRECTIONS: from Hwy 101 in the center of Newport, turn west on N.W. 3rd St. and continue 6 blocks to the ocean.

PREVIOUS PAGE: *Channel House is perched right on this inlet, which is part of the Oregon coastal town of Depoe Bay.*

CHANNEL HOUSE

Endless nautical views

Carved by nature from the rugged Oregon coastline, Depoe Bay is a calm and picturesque body of water favored by sport and commercial fishermen alike. However, navigators pay their dues in the channel that connects the bay to the sea. Nicknamed "The Jaws," it is a treacherous inlet that commands the respect of the most stalwart old salt.

Built high on the rocky shore overlooking this inlet, Channel House commands a magnificent view of all nautical comings-and-goings. A modern, shingled structure, the inn was designed with the sea in mind, and the most desirable accommodations are those that face the water. With sliding glass doors that open onto private balconies, these rooms make guests feel as if they have set to sea. Two of the large oceanfront suites, equipped with full kitchens, working fireplaces, and whirlpool baths, are perfect for two couples traveling together.

Breakfast can be enjoyed in the first-floor dining room, which is decorated with an array of antique brass ships' fittings, or in the privacy of one's room. These include the Cuckoo's Nest, a top-floor, ocean-front suite, the Spouting Horn, with fireplace and ocean-front deck, and The Bridge, a guest room with both ocean and channel views. Charter boats, equipped for a day of serious fishing or for a pleasure cruise, are available at the harbor. Channel House offers all the comforts of a first-class resort with the congeniality of a small ocean hideaway.

CHANNEL HOUSE, P.O. Box 56, Depoe Bay, OR 97341; (503) 765-2140; Paul Schwabe, owner. Bill and Rachel Smith, innkeepers. Six rooms and 3 suites, each with private bath, six with whirlpools, two of which are large ocean-front suites with full kitchens and fireplaces. Rates: $52 to $150. Includes full continental breakfast. Children are welcome, as are well-behaved pets by previous arrangement; Visa, cash, or personal checks.

DIRECTIONS: located on the coast between Newport and Lincoln. Turn west at supermarket onto Ellingson St., just south of the bridge over Depoe Bay.

Perched right on the ocean, you can have breakfast in your room and look at the ever-changing view.

MADISON INN

A family affair

Aided by six offspring who are responsible for everything from bookkeeping to cooking, Kathryn Brandis has created an open and relaxing guest house in her gracious, gabled home.

Perhaps the main reason for the genial atmosphere at the Madison Inn is Kathryn's genius with people. Explains eldest son Matthew: "Mom is incredible. She knows a little something about almost everything and can always spur interesting conversation around the breakfast table."

The spectacular woodwork, moldings, and architectural detail of the house warrant its entry on the National Historic Register.

Located across from a quiet park, the Madison Inn is convenient to both Oregon State University and downtown Corvallis. But the real attraction of the inn is the warmth and hospitality of the Brandis clan.

MADISON INN, 660 SW Madison, Corvallis, OR 97333; (503) 757-1274; Kathryn Brandis, owner; Paige, Matthew, Honore, Mike, Shannon, and Kathleen Brandis, deputy hosts. Spanish and French spoken. Seven rooms, two with private bath, the remaining five rooms sharing three baths. Rate: $50. Includes full breakfast of baked eggs, English muffins, and blended fruit juices. Children welcome; no pets; Belle is the household dog.

DIRECTIONS: from I-5, take the Corvallis-Oregon State exit. Go west ten miles, cross over bridge and take a left onto 6th. Go three blocks, take a right onto Madison, and continue to 7th.

Beautifully preserved woodwork reflects the character of this 1903 Queen Anne.

Natural Pacific Northwest landscaping at its best.

MARJON

Kaleidoscope of color

A path meandering through ferns and over a wooden foot bridge leads to the placid waters of the McKenzie River. Along the way there is a dock for sunbathing and rafts for more adventurous activity. Several spots are inviting to those wishing to relax with some reading or early morning coffee. Over seven hundred rhododendrons and two thousand azaleas provide the colorful background for an extraordinary sculpted acre of trees, shrubs, and flowers. From the tall, century-old apple tree, grafted to have nonconcurrent blooming cycles, to the seven varieties of violets, everything is arranged to provide continuous color throughout spring and summer.

Margie Haas, Marjon's hostess, is as imaginative and dramatic as her landscape. A forest scene with white spruces and life-size deer in the corner of her living room creates the kind of spectacle that only hints at Margie's decorating flair. The living room and dining room are appropriately decorated for the season—leprechauns for St. Patrick's Day, flags and Uncle Sam's top hats on the Fourth of July. Halloween presents special opportunities.

The contemporary house has marvelous river views from windows that tower to twenty-one-foot-high ceilings and extend along half the sixty-foot living room. The master suite opens on to the river on one side and to a formal Japanese garden on the other. French Provincial furniture accented with red velvet, a furry white love seat, and pink sunken tub contribute to this suite's extravagance.

MARJON, 44975 Leaburg Dam Road, Leaburg, OR 97489; (503) 896-3145; Margie Haas, host. Two rooms, both with private baths. Rates: $80 to $100 plus room tax. Includes five-course gourmet breakfast, including hand-sculpted fruit served under a glass dome, cheeses, breads, and eggs. No children; no pets; no smoking in the bedrooms; Visa/MasterCard.

DIRECTIONS: from Eugene take Rte. 126 East for 24 miles. Turn right onto Leaburg Dam Road which crosses over the top of the dam. Proceed for one mile; the road ends at Marjon.

View from the entry hall.

MUMFORD MANOR

Exquisitely detailed

In 1885, Victorian Mumford Manor was built in a farmhouse style on Kings Hill—today, one of Portland's oldest and most prestigious neighborhoods. The Mumford's infectious enthusiasm for the house is apparent, and the interior decoration was mas-

terfully managed by Janis, whose exquisite taste is reflected in every detail.

Betty's Room, named after a woman who grew up in the house, is delightfully decorated with cheerful yellow wallpaper, chintz loveseat, antiques, and balloon curtains on the bay window. At the other end of the hall is the large and lavish Master Suite, running the depth of the house, with windows on three sides. A fireplace, twin chaise lounges, and an ottoman form an enticing sitting area.

Guests are welcome to enjoy the luxurious living room with a 1906 Steinway piano; or the comfy, book-lined library. Those venturing outside will find a brick gazebo surrounded by beautiful gardens— a special delight in spring.

MUMFORD MANOR, 1130 S.W. King, Portland, OR 97205; (503) 243-2443. Janis and Courtland Mumford, owners. Open all year. Four rooms, 2 with private baths and 2 shared. Rates: $80 to $120, including full breakfast elegantly served in the dining room. Children by prior arrangement; no pets; no smoking; Visa/MasterCard/American Express. Resident dog, Esther. Marathon runners Janis and Courtland can direct joggers to local trails. Close to the Performing Arts Center, Art Museum and cosmopolitan shopping. Excellent dining in the area.

DIRECTIONS: *from the north*: take I-405 south off I-5, then exit 2A (Burnside); turn right on Burnside to King Ave; turn left and continue to '1130'. *From the south*: take I-405 north off I-5 and follow to Salmon St. exit; turn left on Taylor and continue to 18th; turn left on 18th, right on Main and continue to King, '1130'.

WHITE HOUSE

A majestic mansion aptly named

Built in 1910 in what was once a resort area for the Portland elite, this grand house belonged to a rags-to-riches lumber tycoon. The mansion, airy and elegantly proportioned, suited his wife's desire to live in a bright and expansive home instead of a dark Victorian-style house prevalent at the time.

Because it closely resembles the President's home in Washington, D.C., neighbors have aptly nicknamed the 7,600-square-foot mansion the "White House." The colossal classic portico with six Doric columns is reminiscent of southern plantation manors. French arched transoms with amber glass, a second-story curved balustrade balcony, and a Mediterranean red tile roof add contrast to the classic style.

The interior is equally dramatic. Graciously tall windows and twelve-foot-high cove ceilings are trimmed with Honduran mahogany.

Hand-painted wall murals in the building's entrance depict rural scenes which recall the grounds at the turn of the century. The huge living room, dining room, and downstairs ballroom indicate the grand entertaining which took place within their walls.

Inkeepers Larry and Mary Hough handle the grandeur with cheery aplomb. Dublin born, Mary was brought up in an English boardinghouse and takes to hostessing quite naturally. Larry enjoys the challenge of the ongoing restoration and clearly enjoys the guests. Theirs is a happy home where visitors are indulged in luxury and jovial, warm hospitality.

WHITE HOUSE, 1914 N.E. 22nd Avenue, Portland, OR 97212; (503) 287-7131; Larry and Mary Hough, hosts. Six rooms, four with private baths. Rates: $66 to $98. Includes a full breakfast that varies between twelve different English-style menus that may include scones, soda bread, oatmeal, and cooked fruits. Children under 12 discouraged; no pets; no smoking; Visa/MasterCard. Seven minutes from downtown business district.

DIRECTIONS: from the north on I-5, take the Coliseum exit. Proceed straight and make a left onto Weidler Blvd. Go to 22nd Ave. and turn left. From the south on I-5, take a right onto Weildler Blvd. Go to 22nd Ave. and turn left.

Owners Larry and Mary Hough.

Left, the Miller Room. Above, the two-story Doric columns dominate the entrance.

MacMASTER HOUSE

Decorated with flair

MacMaster House, with its wonderful high-ceilinged rooms, is one of Portland's more unusual bed and breakfasts, the inspiration being the eclectic tastes of its owner, Cecilia Murphy. After a lengthy career in Oregon radio broadcasting, Cecilia directed her talents to innkeeping in 1986, and has decorated the inn with flair and imagination.

Cecilia attributes her "Out of Africa" period to the dramatic wall mural in the MacMaster suite, depicting zebras galloping across a sun-drenched plain dotted by distant acacia trees. A bamboo four-poster bed, draped with vibrant cotton, and an animal hide throw carpet, adds to the exotic theme. These blend splendidly with the room's classic features such as a gilt-edged mirror over the fireplace, and wonderful antique armchairs. A talented artist, and friend of Cecilia's, has carried the same unique combination of drama, elegance, and whimsy into three other guest rooms, with wall-painting 'headboards' depicting a carousel horse, delicate ferns, and a brilliantly-colored peacock.

A gracious dining room with fireplace, Chinese Chippendale chairs, intricately-carved camphor chest, and a beautifully hand-painted Egyptian geese panel, sets the scene for the guests' breakfast. Fruit juice is accompanied by artistically-presented seasonal fruit, and delicious homemade muffins. Wonderfully creative cooking is produced by Cecilia's kitchen staff, with entrées revolving around regional themes such as Cajun and Southwest cuisine. The food, ambience, and charming, attentive innkeeper make MacMaster House a very special place.

MAC MASTER HOUSE, 1041 S.W. Vista Avenue, Portland, OR 97205; (503) 223-7362. Cecilia Murphy, owner. Open all year. Five guest rooms, all with TV; 4 with fireplaces and queen beds; 2 rooms have private baths; 3 rooms share 1-1/2 baths. Rates: $65 to $95, including full gourmet breakfast. Historic Daniel Campbell House available by calling MacMaster House. Children over 14 welcome; no pets; no smoking inside; Visa/MasterCard/American Express. Magnificent Washington Park, boutiques, galleries and several premier restaurants within walking distance.

DIRECTIONS: *from the north*: take I-405 south off I-5 and exit at Burnside; turn right on Burnside and watch for the Volvo sign on the left; turn left on St. Clair just after the Volvo dealership; turn right on Park Place; go 1 block to Vista and turn left at the light; see MacMaster House on the right. *From the south*: take I-405 north off I-5 and follow to Salmon St. exit; turn left on Taylor and continue to 18th; turn left on 18th and go 1 block; turn right on Salmon; follow Scenic Route signs as Salmon turns into Park Place; turn left at light on Vista and watch for MacMaster House on the right.

HERON HAUS

A little bit of old Hawaii

Perched on the northwest hills of Portland, Julie Keppeler's grand three-story turn-of-the-century house looks out on stunning views of Mount Rainier, Mount St. Helens, and Mount Hood.

Furnished in a classic contemporary style with muted shades, there are touches of antiquity throughout: the family furniture from early days in San Francisco; Indian artifacts, a gift from her stepfather, an authority on the Columbia River Indians; pieces from her mother's unique basket collection; and her own trilobite, ammonite, and brachiopod treasures from her days as a guide at the Natural History Museum in Denver.

Julie Keppeler, the fascinating owner of this bed-and-breakfast inn, lived in Hawaii for twenty-four years, raising her children in a big old plantation house. At the Heron Haus, a wall completely covered with photographs recaptures those days.

Even the guest rooms have Hawaiian names, including Maluhia (peaceful), Manu (bird), and Kulia (Julie's room) named for Julie, the daughter who stripped off four layers of wallpaper before redecorating the room. All of the rooms have ample sitting areas and views of the city and mountains, and two guest suites on the second and third floors offer baths with special extras. One of the showers with original 1904 plumbing offers seven spray spouts.

Breakfast, which starts with freshly cut fruit, is served in the large dining room that extends across one end of the house. A pastry basket with choice offerings such as fresh pumpkin-raisin and cinammon-currant pastries, date nut rolls, and tangy orange rolls are gathered daily from various baker friends in Portland.

Minutes from downtown Portland, there are neighborhood restaurants offering seven different cuisines, as well as boutiques and specialty shops for browsing.

HERON HAUS BED & BREAKFAST INN, 2545 NW Westover Road, Portland, OR 97210; (503) 274-1846; Julie Keppeler, owner. Four guest rooms and 2 master suites, all with private baths, sitting areas, and views of the city. Rates: $85 to $145. Includes a generous continental breakfast. Telephone in each room, computer available, swimming pool on premises. Older children welcome; no pets; no smoking; Visa/MasterCard.

DIRECTIONS: from Hwy. 405, take Everett Street exit to Glisan Street. Take left on Glisan to 24th Street (about 10 blocks) and then a left on Johnson Street for 1 block up to Westover Road. Driveway is ½ block up Westover.

Elaborately Victorian.

JOHN PALMER HOUSE

Dedicated preservationists

The John Palmer House makes it so easy to experience the romance of a bygone era. Victorian niceties such as a complete high tea are offered daily and in addition a fabulous five-course gourmet repast, a private maid and butler for the evening, and an historic tour of Portland by horse and carriage are readily come by.

Owned for the last twenty years by dedicated preservationists Mary and Richard Sauter, the mansion has thrived during their tenure. Featured in magazines such as *Victorian West* and *Sunset*, as well as in "Daughters of Painted Ladies," the 1890 Victorian house was the love-child of builder and contractor John Palmer. As one of the most highly ornamented examples of its kind in the West, each of its unique six gables showcased what Palmer was capable of executing. Its magnificent stained-glass windows were created by the Povey Brothers, the only stained glass-makers between San Francisco and Alaska in that era.

After functioning for thirty years as a music conservatory, the Sauters rescued this important piece of Portland's architectural and cultural history. They have lovingly and painstakingly restored it in this old and recently-reclaimed neighborhood.

The Bridal Suite, a three-room affair, has its own library, sitting room, and porch. A gold velvet 1840s setee, an 1860 Victorian Renaissance Revival pump organ, a marble-topped Eastlake bedroom suite, a lace-covered half-canopy bed, and side chairs covered in a patterned brocade glisten like jewels on the deep pile raisin-wine carpet.

A full gourmet breakfast is served in the Bradbudy-papered dining room that houses an elaborate 1860 grandfather clock once owned by Marconi, and a most unusual sideboard whose doors are inlaid with pewter bas reliefs.

High tea may include cucumber, chicken, or mandarin orange tea sandwiches, fresh fruit, tea cookies, a chocolate fudge torte, a pecan spice, or the house specialty, a hot mushroom tart.

Adjoining the main house is a cottage with a wraparound porch and dormered guest rooms. Each is fitted with brass, oak, or painted bedsteads and up to four or five different wallpapers in one room create visual excitement.

"The only hazard to running the John Palmer House is the guests," quipped the knowledgeable Mary. "We have so much fun with them it's hard to go to bed."

Sumptuously comfortable.

THE JOHN PALMER HOUSE, 4314 North Mississippi Avenue, Portland, OR 97217; (503) 284-5893; Mary and Richard Sauter, hosts. Two suites and one double in main house, two rooms in cottage. Rates: $30 to $95. Includes gourmet breakfast. Dinners Tues. to Sat.; theater weekends. Inquire about children; no pets; no smoking; Visa/MasterCard. High Tea available to public; house tours are conducted Thursday through Sunday. One hour to Columbia Gorge, wine country, and beach. Pick up at airport.

DIRECTIONS: ask for directions when making reservations.

WILLIAM'S HOUSE

All the comforts of home

The rugged beauty of the Columbia River Gorge, with Mt. Adams and Mt. Hood ever present, has attracted generations. Today, acres of cherry and apple orchards, hiking trails, fishing, wind surfing, and endlessly beautiful vistas add to its unique appeal. The Williams family came to this community, at the end of the Oregon Trail, in 1867 and, by selling wagon provisions to the pioneering settlers, built a retailing empire.

Don and Barbara Williams enjoy sharing the home that has been in their family since 1926. On a hillside next to Mill Creek, the Williams House is an oversized beautiful 1899 Victorian. A welcoming and spacious front porch, a gazebo adjacent to a kitchen, and two distinctive second-story porches—one a belvedere tower—make the home charming. Georgian and Victorian antiques are highlighted against vibrant red carpeting. An oil painting depicting an equestrian scene of a young woman off to a hunt, riding a luminescent Arabian stallion, hangs over the piano in the living room. An early nineteenth-century Viole de Gambe and a collection of antique Oriental porcelain are not to be missed. This is a place that feels lived in, and at the same time offers a comfortable elegance.

The area abounds with things to do: white water rafting, year-round fishing in the Columbia River Gorge, and walking tours of The Dalles historic homes and buildings. Of national interest is the Maryhill Museum of Art, opened in 1940 to exhibit native American arts and crafts, Rodin sculpture and drawings, over 100 unique chess sets, Queen Marie of Romania's various collections of jewelry, icons, etc.

WILLIAM'S HOUSE, 608 West 6th Street, The Dalles, OR 97058; (503) 296-2889; Don & Barbara Williams, hosts. Three rooms, one with private bath; two with balconies with views of Klickitat Hills. Rates: $55 to $75 double. Professional rates available. Includes breakfast, beginning with homemade granola, fresh fruits, yogurts, and muffins. Telephones and television on request. Well-behaved children welcome; no pets; smoking in the parlors; Visa/MasterCard/American Express/Discover. Wonderful maps of self-guided driving tours are provided as well as Don's personal tips on the best places with the best views!

DIRECTIONS: from the west, take Rte. 84 at exit 83. Turn left at stop sign onto West 6th St. Cross Trevitt St., cross the bridge, go to end of block and turn right into driveway.

Above, the elegant Master Suite.

FALCON'S CREST

Rustic opulence chalet style

Falcon's Crest is a chalet-style inn nestled in a forest setting below majestic Mt. Hood. Owners Bob and Melody Johnson gave up city jobs in Portland to realize their mutual dream of escaping to a mountain hideaway. Ski Bowl (within walking distance), offers the largest night skiing area in the U.S., and famous Timberline Lodge is just six miles away. However, Falcon's Crest is not only a winter retreat—its natural surroundings also provide a wonderful playground for hiking, golf, white-water rafting, mineral hot springs, fishing, tennis, and swimming.

The Master Suite guest room has an elegant, cherry, four-poster bed, Victorian furnishings, and sliding doors which open onto a secluded private deck (with Jacuzzi). This room boasts a master bath with marvelous amenities such as a Finnish sauna, exercise equipment, and an extra-large shower. The Mexicali Suite is ideal for parties of three or more,

and true to its name, it contains memorabilia collected on the innkeepers' trips to Mexico. Heirlooms from Melody's family are displayed in the Safari and Sophia Suites, while red velvet chairs accent ivory carpeting and a lace comforter in the Cat Ballou Room.

With 5000 square feet of living space, guests may enjoy three expansive common areas, as well as large outdoor decks facing Ski Bowl mountain. The West Loft has a sophisticated air, with velvet upholstery and an imported Italian game table. An ever-expanding library of audio/video tapes make the East Loft a cozy escape. Comfortable furniture and a wood-burning stove in the Great Room, encourage socializing and enjoying pre-dinner appetizers. Breakfast and dinner are both served in the adjoining dining area, with meals presented on one of the hosts' many sets of fine china and stemware.

FALCON'S CREST, 87287 Government Camp Loop Hwy., P.O. Box 185, Government Camp, OR 97028; (503) 272-3403. Bob and Melody Johnson, owners. Open all year. Five suites with private baths. Rates: $85 to $110, including dinner and full breakfast. Children by prior arrangement; no pets; no smoking inside; Visa/MasterCard/American Express. Mystery weekends, corporate packages and private parties can be arranged.

DIRECTIONS: follow Hwy 26 east from Portland to Government Camp. Falcon's Crest is 1/8 mile east from Loop Hwy. interchange on the left, directly across from the BP gas station.

Left, the Fisher Room welcomes you. Above, the meticulously painted lady.

FRANKLIN ST. STATION

Completely Victorian

In 1811, John Jacob Astor's Fur Company established the site that is now Astoria—Oregon's first American settlement. The city borders Washington State at the mouth of the Columbia River, and was strategically situated to become a major trading and shipping center in the early 1800s. Today, it is well known for its numerous Victorian homes—lovingly restored and reminiscent of an earlier, elegant era, of which Franklin St. Station Bed and Breakfast is a fine example.

The dictionary defines "station", as a "regular stopping place." With that meaning in mind, Renée and Jim Caldwell established an inn that would encourage guests to return year after year. "I'm a service-oriented person," says Renée, "and I like to give my guests the very best." She and Jim have

PREVIOUS PAGE: *The incomparable Oregon beach, one of nature's most wonderful creations.*

created an immaculate bed and breakfast through their meticulous renovations.

Each room is richly decorated without being overwhelming. Dark fir trims the inner windows and doorways, and is fashioned into stately Ionic columns jointed by delicate gingerbread spandrels to provide a division between the hall and living room.

In the dining room, where breakfast is served, an oak-mantled fireplace generates a warm atmosphere for those Pacific Northwest winter mornings. Two of Franklin Street's five guest rooms feature decks with Columbia River views; and one room has a private entrance. The individual décor of each guest room reflects Victorian times, with Palladian windows, shirred balloon curtains, iron and brass beds, wicker furniture, appealing wallpapers, and delicate shades of rose, blue, mint, and pink.

FRANKLIN ST. STATION, 1140 Franklin Street, Astoria, OR 97103; (503) 325-4314. Jim and Renée Caldwell, innkeepers. Open all year. Five rooms with private baths, one with TV. Rates: $60 to $85, off-season $50 to $75; includes full breakfast. Two guest rooms acceptable for children; no pets; locked bicycle shed; smoking outside on decks; Visa/MasterCard. Good restaurants in the area, as well as nearby Oregon Coast and Long Beach Peninsula in Washington. Attractions include museums, historic homes walking tour, cycling and popular annual crab/seafood festival in April.

DIRECTIONS: *from south or north:* follow Hwy. 30 to Commercial St.; turn right on 12th St.; continue for 3 blocks and turn right on Franklin. *From the east:* follow Hwy 30 (Marine Drive) to 12th St.; turn left and continue 4 blocks; turn right on Franklin.

Left, top, the Cape Flattery room; bottom, the Cape Disappointment room.

FRANKLIN HOUSE

From dairy farm to painted lady

When Karen Nelson came to Astoria to help at her daughter's Franklin Street Station Bed & Breakfast, she fell in love. So she sold her dairy farm in Salem and returned to Astoria to purchase and renovate one of that city's six-hundred Victorian houses. Now, having turned it into a "painted lady" in five different shades of blue and bright pink, she has taken to innkeeping with uncommon enthusiasm.

Five spacious guest rooms, all with private bathrooms, have brass beds, pretty quilts and curtains, and mauve carpeting throughout the house. There is a double parlor decorated in rose and mauve, and furnished with Victorian pieces that came with the house.

In the formal dining room, Karen serves up scrumptious breakfasts that her guests will remember. Savory French toast, a variety of baked egg dishes in ramekins, and a spinach soufflé (now immortalized in a cookbook), are some of her offerings. In addition, there are delicious muffins baked daily, including such varieties as chocolate-chip, poppyseed, and cheese.

Karen has set up a gift shop in the former den, and sells her own handicrafts as keepsakes. Oil paintings, wood carvings, and painted china dolls are just some of her handiworks.

Two guest rooms in the house have views of the Columbia River, where guests can observe a variety of ships, log-carrying tankers, cruise ships, and pleasure boats. Five blocks from downtown Astoria, the house is within walking distance of the Maritime Museum and Flavel House, an historic mansion.

FRANKLIN HOUSE BED & BREAKFAST INN, 1681 Franklin Ave., Astoria, OR 97103; (503) 325-5044; Karen Nelson, owner. Open all year. Five guest rooms with private baths. Rates: $53 to $75 per room, including full breakfast varying daily. Children welcome; no pets; no smoking; Visa/MasterCard. Recommended restaurants, Pier 11 and Shipinn for seafood. Deepsea fishing for salmon and sturgeon, golfing, Maritime Museum, antiques shops.

DIRECTIONS: two blocks up from Maritime Museum at corner of 17th and Franklin.

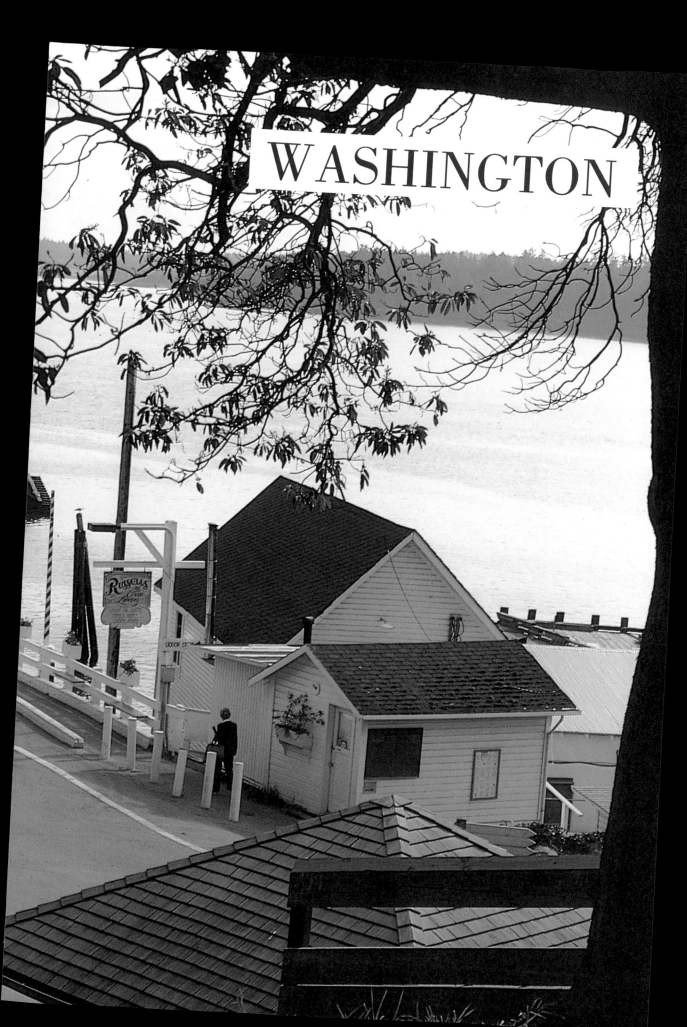

WASHINGTON

INN OF THE WHITE SALMON

Where good taste prevails

This is the place to come for breakfast and to stay several extra days—that is, if you want to taste everything. Innkeepers Roger and Janet Holen and their pastry chef, Alice Strank, serve more than twenty different items daily. Pastries, cakes, breads, and tarts are freshly baked with an assist from two other bakers, and there are orange cream-cheese rolls, pear frangipane, cinnamon toast, flan, Danish bread dough with an almond paste filling, and tart Mirabelle with kirsch-soaked prunes. All are beautiful to behold and incredibly delicious. Since there are six different egg dishes in addition to everything else,

PREVIOUS PAGE: *Washington State Ferry arriving at Orcas Island*

Some of the breakfast treats.

it is impossible to try everything at even two or three breakfasts.

If you can manage to push away from the table, there are exciting white-water rafting tours conducted nearby.

INN OF THE WHITE SALMON, 172 W. Jewett, White Salmon, WA 98672; (509) 493-2335; Roger and Janet Holen, owners. Eighteen rooms, all with private bath, furnished with period antiques in two-story 1930s brick building. Rates: $79 to $198. Includes an extraordinary breakfast of fresh pastries and gourmet egg dishes. Children welcome; smoking permitted but not in dining room; Visa/MasterCard/American Express/Diners Card. Hot tub. Located in the fabulously beautiful Columbia River gorge.

DIRECTIONS: east of Portland on I-84, for 64 miles to exit 64. Follow signs to White Salmon; the inn is towards the end of town on the right.

Left, watch for this ornate sign. Right, the old brass cash register at the front desk.

HAUS ROHRBACH PENSION

Bavarian-style pension

Leavenworth is a reincarnated Bavarian village in the moutainous region of central Washington. From the five porches and decks of Haus Rohrbach, guests have a sweeping vista of the valley and mountains beyond. At night, the view from the balconies of the inn shows the shimmering lights of the town, which cast a magic spell over the valley.

Haus Rohrbach's guest rooms provide simple pleasures: a bit of stenciling, stained pine wainscoting, handmade benches and counter tops, a couple of hooks and a pine shelf with a rod serving as a closet. What is wonderful here is cuddling under down-filled comforters, breathing the fresh mountain air, and listening to the birds and coyotes as the night falls.

The common rooms are large and lodge-like, with built-in benches and long tables for breakfast. There is even a large, carpeted room designated for younger family members. Plenty of coffee, tea, cider, and, sometimes, special sundaes and strudels can be purchased from the Haus kitchen after days of sledding, skiing, horseback riding, or hiking.

HAUS ROHRBACH PENSION, 12882 Ranger Road, Leavenworth, WA 98826; (509) 548-7024; Kathryn & Bob Harrild, hosts. Ten rooms, six with private baths. Rustic, simple decor with fluffy down comforters. Rates: $70 to $120. Includes fabulous breakfast of house specialties such as puffed sourdough pancakes with jams made of local berries. Children are welcome; no pets; smoking outside only; Visa/MasterCard/American Express/Discover. Spa open all year; pool is opened for season. An alpine goat and a family duck roam the lawns.

DIRECTIONS: from Rte. 2 turn onto Ski Hill Drive. Go ½ mile and turn left onto Ranger Road. Follow straight ahead to Pension at end of road.

BROWN'S FARM

A rustic, rural retreat

A few miles from town, the pine pole log home is tucked into a clearing in the woods. From the wraparound porch, you can see the farm's horses, goats, chickens, sheep, rabbits, cats, and dogs. Wendi and the younger Browns are full of tales about the animals, proud to share with travelers the country pleasures of this quiet and unpretentious retreat. Inside the farmhouse there is a large grey hearth lovingly created with stones from the nearby Icicle River Valley. Rag rugs and lots of overstuffed furniture with colorful crocheted throws invite guests to kick off their shoes and curl up for a while.

Heirloom quilts hang on the walls along with other collected Victorian and country memorabilia. Framed in the hall are a dozen or so fascinating labels from the region's apple packing companies that artistically portray local scenes of orchards, mountains, rivers, and wildlife.

After a hearty breakfast of Wendi's inch-thick French toast or four-star omelets served to guests from the country kitchen, guests can explore the miles of hiking trails through the woods or browse through dozens of shops in the nearby Bavarian village of Leavenworth.

BROWN'S FARM, 11150 Highway 209, Leavenworth, WA 98826; (509) 548-7863; Wendi Krieg, host. Three rooms with shared bath. Rates: $60 to $70, $10 extra person. Includes full country breakfast of French toast and sausage or gourmet omelets. Children welcome (bring sleeping bag and pillow); no pets; no smoking in guest rooms; Visa/MasterCard.

DIRECTIONS: from Seattle on Rte. 2, turn left onto Rte. 209. Continue for 1½ miles. The sign is on the right; the driveway on the left. Keep to the left and the driveway will end at the farmhouse.

Dusk is a beautiful time at the farm.

THE MANOR FARM INN

A gentleman's farm

Grazing around the Manor Farm Inn's 1886 two-story white farmhouse are dozens of border Cheviot sheep, long-haired tan Highland cattle, and a herd of Guernsey cows. There are well-groomed horses in the barn and ducks around the pond, which was recently stocked with ten thousand rainbow trout. The twenty-five acres of rolling green meadows surrounding this century-old inn are punctuated by stark white wooden fences.

A rose-covered veranda leads from the parlor, past the guest rooms, and into the dining room. Hors d'oeuvres and sherry are served by the fire in the parlor, furnished with a good sampling of country pine antiques. The dining room's pine chairs were made in Appalachia. At tables covered with pink and white handwoven linens, a gourmet dinner is served by candlelight with classical music in the background. Roast quail, lobster, or flank steak in a plum-pear sauce can be one of the entrées in a five-course meal, and dinner is often completed with port and cheese three hours later.

The meals are prepared by host Robin Hughes, a former restaurateur. Robin believes that guests should encounter an entirely restorative experience here, consisting of elegant surroundings, enticing food, and exquisite serenity. A gentleman's farm, such as this, can provide these pleasures.

THE MANOR FARM INN, 26069 Big Valley Road, N.E., Poulsbo, WA 98370; (206) 779-4628; Robin and Jill Hughes, hosts. Eight guest rooms and 2 cottages, furnished with French country antiques, most with private bath and several with fireplaces. Rates: $90 to $190. Includes juice and scones brought to the room and lavish country breakfast in the dining room a bit later. Sherry and hors d'oeuvres served in the parlor on weekends. Hot tub available. No children; no pets; no smoking; Visa/MasterCard. Gourmet dinners with fixed price are served in the restaurant at one seating. Entire working farm open for guests' pleasure.

DIRECTIONS: from Seattle, take car ferry to Winslow, drive west to Poulsbo, then north on Highway 3 going towards the Hood Canal Bridge. Go about four miles on Rte. 3 until you come to Big Valley Road. Turn right and drive approximately 1.5 miles to the inn. Or take car ferry from Edmonds to Kingston, drive west toward Hood Canal Bridge and continue south on Rte. 3 to Big Valley Road (3 miles from bridge) and turn left, drive 1½ miles to the inn.

The graceful interior of a fine house.

CHAMBERED NAUTILUS

A stately structure

The Chambered Nautilus is a classic colonial structure situated high on a hill in Seattle's university district. With elegant white columns flanking the entryway and supporting the graceful sun porch, the home is at once stately and gracious.

Both the first-floor living room and adjoining dining room, where innkeepers Bunny and Bill Hagemeyer serve breakfast, are equipped with working fireplaces. Breakfast might include apple quiche, pumpkin-blueberry muffins, or peach muffins prepared by Bunny, who studied with the legendary James Beard. One of Bunny's breakfast recipes was named Recipe of the Year in a national competition among 1500 inns.

Each of the large and airy bedrooms is furnished with thoughtfully coordinated beds and bureaus, and several rooms open onto private porches that overlook the ivy-covered hillside and colorful gardens. Throughout, contemporary graphic prints and delicate watercolors decorate the walls.

After breakfast, visitors may spend the day exploring the pleasures of Seattle and the surrounding area.

CHAMBERED NAUTILUS, 5005 22nd Avenue, N.E., Seattle, WA 98105; (206) 522-2536; Bunny and Bill Hagemeyer, hosts. Six rooms with private and shared baths. Rates: $59 to $95. Includes full breakfast of scones, muffins or coffee cake, fresh fruits and yogurts, quiche, waffles, and baked egg dishes. Children under twelve by special arrangement; no pets; cigarette smoking on porches only; all major credit cards. The pets of the house are 2 loving black labs, regularly spoiled by guests. Seminars, business meetings, and receptions can be accommodated. The house is accessible only by a flight of steps.

DIRECTIONS: from I-5, take 50th St. East exit. Proceed about 1½ miles and turn left onto 20th Ave. N.E. Go four blocks and take a right onto 54th St. N.E. Proceed down a steep hill and turn right onto 22nd St. N.E.

SEATTLE AR

Views and Visions in the
Pacific Northwest
June 7 – September 2

Alfredo Jaar
August 16–September 30

OPEN HOURS   SUNDAYS 12 – 5 P.M.
TUESDAY – SATURDAY 10 A
THURSDAY EVENING

USEUM

Welcome to the
Seattle Art Museum

Members admitted free
Adults $2.00
Students/Seniors $1.00
Children under 6   free
Every Thursday   free

Hours:
Sunday   noon – 5 pm
Tuesday – Saturday   10 am – 5 pm
Thursday   10 am – 9 pm
Closed Monday

WELCOME

SALISBURY HOUSE

Gracious elegance

Located in the impressive Capital Hill section of Seattle, Salisbury House represents all that is gracious and elegant about the area. Its wraparound porch invites you to relax with a cool refreshment on a hot summer day, or perhaps you would prefer a stroll through the private gardens in back.

On entering Salisbury House, Mary Wiese and daughter Cathryn welcome you to their unique and popular inn. They have decorated each of the four guest rooms with inviting individuality, designed to make maximum use of large, sunny windows.

If you are staying in the Lavender room (one of Salisbury's most spacious), you will be pampered by a queen-size bed with a luscious lavender and pink down comforter, a cushioned window seat overlooking the garden, and comfy wicker chairs. Larger still, the Rose room is a favorite, with an enticing canopy bed, antique oak armoire, and a wonderful walk-in dressing closet.

PREVIOUS PAGE: *Art deco magnificence in Volunteer Park, where Seattle's only camels quietly rest in perpetuity.*

You can take advantage of Salisbury's central location to tour America's "most livable city," major attractions within walking distance.

SALISBURY HOUSE, 750 16th Ave. E., Seattle, WA 98112; (206) 328-8682. Mary and Cathryn Wiese, innkeepers. Open all year. Four rooms sharing 2 large bathrooms, 1 with double basins and shower/tub, the other with stall shower and 6 ft. tub. Rates: $65 to $75 single, $70 to $80 double. Includes full breakfast with no meats, seasonal fruit, juice, freshly baked rolls, homemade jams and egg entrées. Children over 12; no pets; no smoking inside; all major credit cards; some Spanish spoken. Resident cats, Jane and Emily.

DIRECTIONS: *from the north*: take exit 168A (Boylston/Roanoke) off I-5; turn left over the freeway; drive 2 blocks to 10th Ave. E.; turn right on 10th proceeding about 1 mile to Aloha; turn left and continue to 16th Ave. E. where Salisbury House is on southeast corner. *From the south*: take exit 164 (Madison Ave.) off I-5; turn right on Madison and proceed about 1-3/4 miles to 15th Ave. E.; turn left and continue to Aloha; turn right and go one block.

BEECH TREE MANOR

A dynamic woman beloved by guests

An extensive art collection.

Presided over by a colorful and artistic proprietress, Beech Tree Manor offers the traveler modern amenities in a genteel setting. For four years, Virginia Lucero has held court at this restored turn-of-the-century turquoise mansion on historic Queen Anne Hill amid grounds planted with foxglove, delphinium, roses, and irises.

The interior of the pink-and-beige-trimmed clapboard house is dressed in Laura Ashley wallpaper and fabrics, and has an English country house feeling. Original wood, beamed ceilings, and embossed tin walls above the wood paneling in the living room add to the effect. Beautiful old delicate lace covers tables; oriental rugs cover hardwood floors. A recent guest from the *Chicago Tribune* immediately noted the owner's fabulous bicoastal collection of abstract art collected over twenty-five years.

The emphasis in the dinning room is on *food.* Virginia, trained by a Maryland chef, is no slouch in the kitchen. Gourmet breakfasts await guests

each morning. Eggs Pacifica—eggs and shrimp in capered cream sauce over toast points—French toast baked in rum-raisin ice cream, warm fresh scones stuffed with raspberries, blueberries, or strawberries in a gingered cream are perennial favorites. Some visitors come to Seattle just to have breakfast here.

An extra feature is Virginia's antique lace shop where vintage bed and table linens are prettily displayed and sold. English and Scottish coverlets, pillow cases, tablecloths, and squares are bought up as mementos by guests.

Born in Seattle, Virginia is well-read and well-traveled. Guests simply adore her and women often emulate her as a role model—a woman who started from scratch and became a success.

She is so well-liked that it is not unusual for guests to invite her to a movie or out for a drink. She recently attended a former guest's wedding in Dallas.

THE BEECH TREE MANOR, 1405 Queen Anne Avenue North, Seattle, WA 98109; (206) 281-7037; Virginia Lucero, owner. Six guest rooms, 3 with private baths, 3 with shared baths. Open all year. Rates: $55 to $75 a couple; $45 to $70 single. Includes a gourmet breakfast. Children over 2 welcome; dogs accepted; smoking restricted; all major credit cards. Walk to Space Needle, opera, ballet, symphony, theater, and restaurants. English bulldog. Chief White Cloud, on premises.

DIRECTIONS: inquire when making reservations.

Breakfast includes "Larry's eggs"—individual soufflés of egg, cheese, cream, and broccoli, perfected by Roberta's son.

ROBERTA'S

Relax in comfort

Around the turn of the century, Seattle was booming in the wake of the Klondike gold rush. Some of the more affluent families moving to the city began settling in the vicinity of Capitol Hill. Roberta's, a

handsome 1904 residence, is an example of the various roomy and gracious homes that still survive in this house-proud neighborhood.

Roberta's namesake, owner, manager, and inn-keeper, Roberta Barry, is a long-time Seattle resident who has been welcoming guests to her bed and breakfast for the past seven years. Exceptionally relaxed, she ensures that everyone enjoys their stay.

The interior of the house is comfortable and uncluttered, with a homey atmosphere. Madrona, Rosewood, Peach, and Plum guest rooms on the second floor feature comfortable queen-sized beds, down comforters, antiques, and locally crafted ceramic sinks in the bathrooms.

ROBERTA'S, 1147 Sixteenth Ave. E., Seattle, WA 98112; (206) 329-3326. Roberta Barry, owner. Open all year. Five guest rooms with queen beds; 4 with private baths and 1 with bath across hall. Rates: $75 to $95, including full breakfast. Children over 12; no pets; no smoking inside; Visa/MasterCard/American Express/Diner's Club. Resident cat, Wally. Seattle Art Museum 1 block.

DIRECTIONS: *from the south*: take exit 166 (Olive Way) off I-5; follow up the hill to 15th Ave. E.; turn left and continue to Prospect; turn right and then left on 16th. *From the north*: take exit 168A (Roanoke) off I-5; turn left at the stoplight and continue to 10th Avenue E.; turn right and follow 10th Ave. E. to E. Boston; turn left and follow until it becomes 15th Ave. E.; turn left on E. Highland and right on 16th Ave. E.

GASLIGHT INN

An exciting blend of old and new

Gaslight Inn was built by Dwight Christianson in 1906, and remained in his family until Trevor Logan and Steve Bennett became owners in 1983. During the process of converting the impressive mansion into a bed and breakfast, Trevor and Steve have maintained its original style while introducing contemporary conveniences.

The home was designed as an example of the various construction features that purchasers could choose from when selecting house plans. The ground floor is a 'four square' design with a grand center hall, two roomy parlors on either side, a library, and a dining room to the rear. Windows feature

Left, top, the magnificent oak staircase; bottom, a traditional guest room. Below, the swimming pool in the back garden.

beautiful beveled glass, while the upstairs landing is illuminated by a decorative stained-glass panel. Throughout, gleaming oak is fashioned into pillars, paneling, fireplace mantels, and bookcases.

At the turn of the century, when electricity was first introduced, many homes had a combination of gas and electric power. Gaslight Inn retains this unique feature, and derives its name from handsome brass chandeliers with gas flames above glass-shaded lights.

The nine guest rooms are decorated in styles ranging from turn-of-the-century antique, to rustic country and classic contemporary. Much of the midwest oak furniture came from Steve's family, and is typical of items produced for Sears in the early part of this century. The quilts from Trevor's Canadian grandmother go very well with the rich, luster of walnut beds and dressers, or with sleek, modern furnishings. Rooms at the back of the house share wonderful cityscape panoramas of Seattle.

Continental breakfast includes mouth-watering homemade scones and croissants, seasonal fruit, delicious Starbuck's coffee, fresh-squeezed orange juice, and homemade jams, all set out on the sideboard of the elegant oak dining room.

Original Pacific northwest artwork is highlighted, and adds local flavor to most rooms.

GASLIGHT INN, 1727 15th Avenue, Seattle, WA 98122; (206) 325-3654. Trevor Logan and Steve Bennett, innkeepers. Open all year. Nine guest rooms, 5 with private baths and 4 shared; TV and refrigerators in each. Rates: $58 to $94, including continental breakfast. Swimming pool; no children; no pets; smoking allowed except in dining room and adjacent parlor; Visa/MasterCard/American Express. Great bistros, cafes and city night spots easily accessible.

DIRECTIONS: *from the north*: take exit 166 (Denny Way); turn left on Denny; continue to 12th Ave. and turn right; go 1 block and turn left; proceed for 3 blocks turning right onto 15th to '1727' (corner Howell). *From the south*: take the Madison St. exit off I-5; turn right on Madison and continue approximately 15 blocks to 15th Ave.; turn left and go three blocks to corner to '1727' (corner Howell).

RIDGEWAY HOUSE

A mecca for tulip lovers

Serendipity brought Donna Huckstadt to open her home to visitors. She had been presented with a gift of her first stay at a bed and breakfast; and when forced to change occupations and lifestyles, she determined that Ridgeway House was the perfect solution. Donna has turned this 1928 home into an inviting getaway.

Unlike other bed and breakfasts in the Skagit Valley, Ridgeway was the first brick house, and was formerly part of a large dairy farm. Built prior to roads or dikes, the original owner transported all building materials, possessions, and his family, along the 'ridgeway'—the high ground above the flood plain. Today, the spacious, yellow brick house is sheltered on one side by 65-year-old poplars, and is surrounded by working farms.

Everything about the immaculate interior at Ridgeway House is fresh and airy, with sparkling oak floors in the living and dining rooms, white furniture, gleaming glass, a warm fireplace, and delicate area carpets. Each guest room has a uniquely

Left, top, a sumptuous ground floor guest room; bottom, the sitting room seen from the dining room.

Some guest rooms have bathtubs right in the room—a special feature.

distinct décor ranging from apricot linens and wicker, to brass beds, or a four-poster with a floral comforter in soft tones.

Donna is justifiably proud of her breakfasts, served in the cherry dining room. Fresh-squeezed orange juice in graceful goblets, and pears with rum sauce topped with whipped cream could be the prélude to quiche with sausage, egg crêpes with crab thermidor, or French toast smothered in Grand Marnier orange butter. Wholesome, home-baked muffins are part of every breakfast.

Ridgeway House is ideally located between Mt. Vernon and La Conner. In springtime, the vast flatlands are blanketed with vibrant red, yellow, pink, and purple tulips, which attract thousands of visitors to the area. It is a photographer's dream, and a joy to the senses. Perhaps the best way to view this brilliant spectacle is by bicycle—a popular pastime on the valley backroads.

RIDGEWAY HOUSE, 1292 McLean Road, Mt. Vernon, WA 98273; (206) 428-8068. Donna Huckstadt, innkeeper. Open all year. Five rooms, 2 with private baths and queen beds; 3 share 2 bathrooms. Rates: $45 to $75, including full gourmet breakfast. Book weekends one year in advance for tulip festival. Children by prior arrangement; no pets; no smoking inside; Visa/MasterCard. Dining in nearby Mt. Vernon, La Conner, and Chuckanut Drive.

DIRECTIONS: take exit 226 off I-5 and go east on Kincaid; turn right on 3rd and continue across the Skagit River; turn left on Wall, which becomes McLean; proceed west on McLean for 3-1/2 miles.

WHITE SWAN GUEST HOUSE

A fantasy farmhouse

Peter Goldfarb fell in love with the fertile Skagit Valley when he came to visit a few years ago, and immediately bought an 1898 Victorian farmhouse. An English country garden, surrounding the White Swan Inn, is the creation of this former children's-wear designer from the Big Apple. "I've always wanted a farmhouse, and the fun of having it was creating a bed and breakfast from a house that was destined to be plowed under," Peter explains. "I loved the idea and the romance of a farm."

The White Swan has allowed Peter to pursue his rural dream. Located on a quiet country road, just six miles from the fishing village of La Conner, this inn represents an image of everyone's fantasy farmhouse. Towering poplars along the driveway lead to a yellow house with white trim, picket fences, wicker furniture on the back porch, and the dazzling profusion of blossoms in Peter's ever-expanding gardens.

The attractive rooms are painted in shades of yellow, rose, and pink, and have lots of windows—presenting a quality of airy, open comfort. Each of the three guest rooms on the second floor has a special kind of country appeal. One room has an inviting window seat in a lace-curtained turret, where the original owner used to watch boats on the Skagit River. Although antiques are an integral part of the White Swan, they are neither ornate nor overwhelming. A delightful, contemporary guest cottage is at the edge of wide fields, where graceful, wintering white swans captivate bird watchers.

Peter's overflowing enthusiasm for the region is contagious, and he shares his knowledge of the attractions, providing guests with many choices and opportunities for exploring La Conner, nearby San Juan Islands, Deception Pass State Park, and Whidbey Island.

THE WHITE SWAN GUEST HOUSE, 1388 Moore Road, Mt. Vernon, WA 98273; (206) 445-6805. Peter Goldfarb, owner. Open all year. Three guest rooms share two large bathrooms; separate 2-storey guest cottage with queen bed, double foldout futon and kitchen. Rates: $65 to $150, including generous country continental breakfast. Children and pets allowed in guest cottage; no smoking inside; Visa/MasterCard. Resident dogs, Chester and Shadow. Good dining within easy driving distance, emphasizing seafood. Cycling, art galleries, antiques shops, famous spring tulip festival.

DIRECTIONS: take exit 221 off I-5 (Conway-La Conner); head west on Fir Island Road for 5 miles; at the yellow blinking light, go straight on Moore Road for 1 mile; White Swan sign on right.

Three antique clocks decorate the dining room.

CASTLE BED AND BREAKFAST

Lavish antiques

Old Fairhaven, a district of Bellingham, is home to the Castle, a distinctive and imposing landmark boldly painted mauve with deep plum trim. Original owner Jim Wardner was a flamboyant promoter, whose fortunes rose and fell in pursuits as diverse as mining, cat-fur farming, and real estate.

Since they bought the Castle fifteen years ago, Larry and Gloria Harriman have been restoring this century-old treasure to its former glory. With twelve-thousand square feet and twenty-three rooms, their task is enormous, but the Harrimans have worked wonders.

Each of the Castle's three guest rooms has outstanding views of Bellingham Bay, and at night the lights of Fairhaven twinkle below. The Cupola is a very spacious room with red carpeting, antiques, and a queen-sized bed placed in the cupola window.

Left, top, the upstairs hall displays an inlaid credenza and a mahogany cased grandfather clock; bottom, an elaborate shared bathroom.

From its carved oak bedstead, Bayview has sweeping views of the bay through many lace-curtained windows. The Folk Art room, with its twin beds, is decorated in an eclectic display of masks, carved wooden animals, jewelry, statues, and African-motif wallpaper.

Larry and Gloria have decorated the ground floor of the Castle with a lavish collection of authentic English, German, Russian, and Norwegian antiques acquired from years in the antiques business. Only a house with such enormous rooms could accommodate the massive proportions of the many wonderful cabinets, desks, sideboards, chairs, tables, and lamps.

An imposing Russian china cabinet dominates one end of the regal dining room, where guests eat breakfast sitting on eighteenth-century oak chairs, each with uniquely carved designs and tapestry covers.

THE CASTLE B & B, 1103 15th Street, Bellingham, WA 98225; (206) 676-0974. Larry and Gloria Harriman, owners. Open all year. Three rooms, 1 with private bath, 2 sharing an extravagant period style bathroom. Rates: $65 to $85. No children; no pets; no smoking; Visa/MasterCard. Dining within walking distance. Activities include skiing, boating, hiking, fishing, diving, tennis and day trip ferries to the San Juan Islands. Alaska ferry terminal and international airport nearby.

DIRECTIONS: take exit 250 off I-5 and go west on Old Fairhaven Pkwy; turn right on 14th and continue to Knox St.; turn right to The Castle at Knox and 15th.

DOWNEY HOUSE

What a Christmas present!

When Jim and Kay Frey were in their mid-twenties, an incredible opportunity presented itself—a "giveaway" mansion.

Just around Christmas time, the owners of a heritage country home offered it free to anyone who would move it off their property—Jim and Kay accepted the challenge. They transported the home three miles down the road to where it now sits on a gentle slope with views across a broad valley to the distant foothills of the Cascade Mountains. Since receiving that amazing Christmas gift, the Freys have raised their family in the spacious home and have since converted it into one of La Conner's most attractive bed and breakfasts.

Jim and Kay are gracious and welcoming inn-keepers, who share the evening conversation around a large dining room table while guests enjoy the inn's trademark—blackberry pie with ice cream. They never seem to tire of describing how they acquired the house, slowly began the remodeling process, and assembled a collection of antiques which they refinished themselves. Many pieces were brought from Nebraska, Jim's home state, while most of the other furnishings were purchased in and around La Conner.

Left,
An antique oak pump organ dominates the sitting room.

Hosts Kay and Jim Frey.

Lining the stairway walls, sepia-toned historic photos depict La Conner and noted landmarks as they were one hundred years ago, side-by-side with modern photos of the same subjects. Guest rooms are named after both Jim's and Kay's families, while a separate suite honors Peter Downey, the man who built the house. The large McCormick room displays the wedding shoes and nightgown of Kay's grand-mother, as well as her trunk addressed to "Washington Territory". It is a gracious room with tall bay windows and a brass and iron bed. The Randles, Berglund, and Frey rooms are smaller, but equally as charming, with handsome cherry, oak, or brass beds, and elegant armoires or dressers. Some rooms display paintings by renowned local sporting artist, David Hagerbaumer.

DOWNEY HOUSE, 1880 Chilberg Road, La Conner, WA 98257; (206) 466-3207. Jim and Kay Frey, innkeepers. Open all year. Five guest rooms, 3 with private baths, 2 shared. Rates: $75 to $95, including full breakfast. Young children during mid-week only; no pets; no smoking; Visa/MasterCard. Excellent restaurants within short driving distance. La Conner is one of the oldest towns in Washington State and designated a National Historic District "noted for its preservation and restoration".

DIRECTIONS: *from the north*: take exit 230 off I-5 and go west on Hwy 20 toward Anacortes; turn left on Best Road and go south 5 miles, past 2 stop signs, to Downey House on right side of road. *From the south*: take exit 221 off I-5 continuing for 6.5 miles through Conway towards La Conner on Fir Island Road; Downey House on left side of road (Chilberg).

CLIFF HOUSE

An architectural masterpiece

Cliff House is simply breathtaking! Philip Johnson, the renowned architect who selected Cliff House to receive an AIA award in 1980, was particularly taken with the large open atrium rising through the center of the house and the profusion of natural light that floods the interior. As its name indicates, Cliff House sits on a bluff above the sea—its large windows revealing the drama of the Olympic Mountains in the distance, high above Admiralty Inlet. Ships steaming into Seattle pass offshore, and blood-red sunsets reflecting off the water, make this an unusually romantic and spectacularly beautiful place.

The interior of the house blends rugged stone with cedar structural beams, a luxurious sunken living room, plush carpeting, primitive art, delicate paintings, and nature photographs taken by the hostess, Peggy Moore. Because the house is so much a part of her life, Peggy and Walter, her co-host, are exhilarated by their guests' enthusiasm. They rent the one-bedroom house in its entirety, to one or two couples at a time. In

addition, there is now a cottage, Seacliff, for rent separately to another couple.

CLIFF HOUSE, 5440 Windmill Road, Freeland, WA 98249; (206) 321-1566; Peggy and Walter, hosts. The entire house is for rent. Rates: $185 for 1 couple, $385 for 2 couples; cottage $145 for 1 couple. Includes continental breakfast. Cannot accommodate children or pets; non-smokers are preferred; no credit cards. Stairway to the beach and hot tub on outside deck in a 13-acre secluded wooded setting.

DIRECTIONS: from the Whidbey Island/Mukilteo Ferry, drive 11 miles on Rte. 525 and turn left onto Bush Point Rd. (after pizza parlor on left and Book Bay on right). Proceed 1¼ miles and turn left on Grigware Rd. The driveway is on the right.

CHANNEL HOUSE

Spectacular views of the San Juan Islands

From the large outdoor hot tub behind this house you can get a panoramic view of the sunset over Puget Sound and the boats navigating the Guemes Channel. Built in 1902, this three-story bungalow is just minutes from the ferry.

Furnished throughout with turn-of-the-century pieces, the guest rooms are large and airy and have antique brass, mahogany, and canopied beds. The main floor will make guests feel perfectly at home. There is a library and music room with its own fireplace, an inviting formal living room, and a tiled solarium filled with all manner of greenery. A full breakfast of fresh fruit, home-baked breads, and an assortment of egg dishes is served in the sunny dining room.

A large French country style barn is on the drawing board, and will house a host of activities, including a variety of art courses and concerts.

CHANNEL HOUSE, 2902 Oakes Avenue, Anacortes, WA 98221. (206) 293-9382. Dennis and Patricia McIntyre, hosts. Four rooms with two shared baths. Rates: $55 to $65. Includes a full breakfast of fruits, baked breads, and egg dishes. No children under twelve; no pets; no smoking; Visa/MasterCard. Outdoor hot tub. Bicycle rentals.

DIRECTIONS: from I-5, take Highway 20 west and follow signs to Anacortes Ferry, which will put you on Oakes Avenue. Follow the numbers to 2902 Oakes and Channel House is on the right, waterside.

Built by an Italian count in 1902.

KANGAROO HOUSE

The romance of island living

Having traveled and eaten throughout most of Europe and Latin America, Jan and Mike Russillo know how things are done. They brought that know-how to this large, craftsman-style home and combined it with the romance of island living. Hospitality comes to them naturally, making them popular innkeepers and turning their place into a most congenial spot to stay.

Features include a scrumptious three-course breakfast, a game room for backgammon and puzzles, a large sitting room with stone fireplace for reading and conversation, and sunny, flower-filled decks for pure relaxation. "When six or eight strangers get to playing Trivial Pursuit and drinking fresh cider—it's a real good feeling," muses Jan.

Fine restaurants, quaint shops, and galleries abound on Orcas Island, and there is swimming, fishing, and hiking at nearby Moran State Park. There are also kayak excursions for viewing seals, otters, and eagles.

KANGAROO HOUSE, North Beach Road on Orcas Island, P.O. Box 334, Eastsound, WA 98245; (206) 376-2175; Mike and Jan Russillo, hosts. Three guest rooms with shared baths; 2 suites, each with private baths. Rates: $55 to $100. Includes a full breakfast. Children welcome; no pets; smoking limited to outside areas; Visa/MasterCard. Ask about special winter rates.

DIRECTIONS: the island can be reached by air from Seattle or Bellingham, or via the Washington State Ferry, which has seven departures each day in season from Anacortes and takes about 1¼ hrs. Once on Orcas follow the ferry traffic and the signs into Eastsound. Take a left at the only traffic light onto North Beach Rd. and go about a mile. The house is on the left. Complimentary airport pickups.

TURTLEBACK FARM

A lovingly restored old farmhouse

PHOTOGRAPH JEFFREY P. BUCHNER

The kind of breakfast that sticks to your ribs.

In the shadow of Turtleback Mountain, on eighty acres of forest and farmlands, Turtleback Farm Inn is set on Orcas Island, the jewel of the San Juans. The farmhouse was discovered by Bill and Susan Fletcher, two Californians in search of a summer home on Orcas. Falling in love with the charming but needy house, the Fletchers ended up having to buy the whole valley to get the one-hundred-year-old wood-frame house. Now lovingly restored, it reflects the sensitive artistry of its owners.

All of the rooms are awash in Victorian colors—jade, taupe, sage, and clotted cream—and offset by local Northwest fir floorboards, trim, and wainscoting. Each of the seven guest rooms has its own charm: The Nook, as snug and as cozy as a ship's cabin; the Meadow View with lovely antique furnishings and a private deck; the Orchard View with a special panorama of the orchard and sheep pasture. The Garden View, overlooking the English country flower garden, has prize-winning irises planted by a Bellingham radio announcer who insisted that they belonged in the Fletchers' garden. And so they do!

There are appointments rescued from times and places gone by: a basin and glass shelf from the Empress Hotel in Victoria, crystal doorknobs from the old Seattle Savoy Hotel, and a framed newspaper ad for the 1933 film *Tarzan the Fearless*. Buster Crabbe, the legendary Tarzan as well as the immortal Flash Gordon, was Susan's father.

Breakfast always consists of fresh seasonal fruit—the Turtleback's own apples in the fall and the island's berries in the summer—and cereals that include Susan's own granola, so popular she has recipes printed to distribute to guests.

TURTLEBACK FARM GRANOLA
4 cups rolled oats
3 cups whole wheat flour
1 cup white flour (unbleached)
1 cup shredded coconut

Left bottom, indoor-outdoor living at its rural best.

1 cup chopped nuts
1 cup wheat germ
½ cup cornmeal
1 cup oil
2 tbs. honey
1 cup warm water
1 tablespoon salt (may be omitted)

Mix all ingredients well and spread in two 9″ × 12″ pans. Bake 300° stirring often to prevent scorching, approximately 2 hours.

This is followed by "The Cook's Choice"—quiche, crêpes, or corn waffles, served up with succulent ham, bacon, or sausage.

Acres of verdant meadows, sweet-smelling woods, a sweeping pasture, a trout-stocked pond, a nine-hole golf course, and above all, heavenly peace are to be found here.

TURTLEBACK FARM INN, Route 1, Box 650, Eastsound, Orcas Island, WA 98245; (206) 376-4914; Bill and Susan Fletcher, hosts. Seven rooms, all with private baths. Individual heat-control thermostats. Rates: $65 to $145. Includes hearty breakfast. Children by special arrangement only; no pets; no smoking indoors; Visa/MasterCard. Forests, lakes, quaint villages within easy driving or biking; Moran State Park, and Doe Bay for mineral baths and steam saunas.

DIRECTIONS: inquire when making reservations.

Left, a ground floor suite. Above, a skylight-lit attic suite with sleigh bed.

INN AT SWIFTS BAY

Island hospitality

Lopez, known as the "Friendly Isle", is one of the quietest San Juan islands, with acres of rolling farmland and forest. It also boasts more public beach access than other islands in the archipelago.

Between Swifts and Shoal Bay is a former summer house which makes the perfect bed and breakfast. Chris Brandmeir and Robert Herrmann have converted the tudor-style structure into a wonderfully relaxing inn, which combines luxury, comfort, elegance, and subtle pampering. For the inn brochures they have adopted a pineapple emblem—recognized for hundreds of years as the symbol of American hospitality, and well suited to the atmosphere created by Robert and Chris.

The day begins with a sumptuous breakfast served at four tables on a cozy dais, with a bay window overlooking the garden. A blend of pineapple juice, fresh peaches, lime, and banana makes a delightful morning beverage. Muffins are baked every day and entrées include apple, ham, and brie omelet, shrimp soufflé with lobster sauce, eggs Dungeness, hazelnut waffles with crème fraîche and seasonal fruit, quiche Lorraine, and other culinary delights.

There are many entertaining things to do around the inn, such as relaxing in the secluded hot tub, sunning on the patio, choosing from an extensive collection of videos, books, and music tapes in the library, or socializing in the living room, in front of the fireplace. Further away is an acre of private beach with good clamming.

At day's end, four attractive rooms accommodate guests in restfully decorated surroundings. Each overlooks the tree-filled gardens and presents its own distinct, well-appointed character.

INN AT SWIFTS BAY, Route 2, Box 3402, Port Stanley Road, Lopez Island, WA 98261; (206) 468-3636. Robert Herrmann and Chris Brandmeir, owners. Open all year. Four guest rooms, all with queen beds; 2 share a bath; 2 are suites with private baths and separate sitting areas. Rates: $75 with shared bath; $95 to $115 for suites. Full breakfast; every attempt will made to accommodate special dietary needs. No children; no pets; no smoking inside; Visa/MasterCard; Portuguese and German spoken. Resident dog, Max. Fine dining in the village 4 miles away. Whale watching excursions in season, cycling, beachcombing and swimming.

DIRECTIONS: take San Juan Islands ferry from Anacortes to Lopez Island (first stop); head towards the Village and take the first major left onto Port Stanley Road opposite Odlin Park entrance; continue for approximately 3/4 mile to '3402' on the right. Pickup service by prior arrangement at ferry, airstrip or seaplane dock.

OLD CONSULATE INN (F.W. Hastings House)

Tower views of Port Townsend

Carefully maintained as a family residence until it became an inn, the house never required restoration, and today it is on the National Register of Historic Landmarks. Built in 1889 by one of the founders of Port Townsend, Frank Hasting's home can be described as a Queen Anne Victorian with an Edwardian influence.

Two elegant turrets, a wraparound porch, a quarter-turn staircase, Italian ceramic fireplaces, hand-rubbed oak woodwork, and an Italian blown glass grape chandelier are original to the house. The old furniture is no longer here, but the house has been decorated with a sensitivity to the period and to its architectural lines and scale. Everything is simple and elegant and looks as if it belongs.

Rising three stories, the turret at the front corner of the house creates delightful circular alcoves in the main floor parlor and in the master and third-floor bedrooms. Each of the upstairs alcoves serves as a charming sitting room for the bedrooms, and each has a marvelous view of Admiralty Inlet.

The lower garden level has a game and billiard room, with a special conversation area arranged around a wood stove.

OLD CONSULATE INN (F. W. HASTINGS HOUSE) 313 Walker at Washington, Port Townsend, WA 98368; (206) 385-6733; Rob and Joanna Jackson, owners. Eight rooms, including 2 bridal suites; private baths. Rates: $59 to $130. Winter rates slightly less. Includes full breakfast of fruit juices, egg dishes, meats, cheeses, home baked breads and cakes. Children over twelve; no pets; no smoking; Visa/MasterCard.

DIRECTIONS: from Seattle take the ferry to Winslow and follow the signs to Hood Canal Bridge. Cross bridge and follow signs to Port Townsend. After the first set of lights turn left onto Washington St. Go one block to the top of the hill and the house is on the corner.

A tower guest room.

LIZZIE'S

It is easy to feel at home

Patti and Bill Wickline, the new owners of Lizzie's, are "people persons" and enjoy talking to guests of an evening or over morning coffee. Recent guests include a husband and wife, both professors from Alaska, a Russian psychologist, and the owner of a 1,000 acre maple sugar farm in Canada. The Wicklines feel they are promoting good international relations via bed and breakfast.

Lizzie's—named after Lizzie Grant, the colorful widow of a Port Townsend sea captain—shines with glistening new paint, plumbing, wiring, sprinklers, bathrooms, and kitchen. The Italianate Victorian building is admirably furnished with Queen Anne chairs, a Victorian leather chesterfield sofa, a brilliant red carpet, and a Knabe grand piano. Silk hangings from the Broadway production of *The Flower Drum Song* hang on either side of a marble fireplace. The inn is not

This 1880s Italianate Victorian is part of Port Townsend's legacy.

pretentious, and it is easy to feel at home here.

Breakfasts are served at a twelve-foot oak table in the kitchen, amid welcome informality. Cast-iron muffin tins, a Chinese bamboo steamer, a wire egg basket, and other cooking utensils hang from a handmade iron pot rack overhead. There is a big old hotel stove with six burners, two ovens, and three broilers that is used to serve up a full breakfast that may include baked eggs, crêpes, or egg-cheese puffs.

There is also a brand of Lizzie's toiletries. The custom-made apricot soaps and lotions are a trademark. Altogether this is a most pleasant place to visit.

LIZZIE'S, 731 Pierce Street, Port Townsend, WA 98368; (206) 385-4168; Patti and Bill Wickline, owners. Eight rooms tastefully decorated, private and shared baths. Open all year. Rates: $55 to $98. Includes generous full breakfast. Children over ten; no pets; Visa/MasterCard. Lizzie's brand of soaps and lotions available for purchase.

DIRECTIONS: from the Port Townsend Ferry take a right onto Water St., in one block take a left onto Taylor St. At the fountain, turn left onto Washington St. Proceed up the hill and turn right onto Pierce and proceed six blocks. From the south, at the third Port Townsend stoplight take a left onto Taylor St. and proceed as above.

Tasteful Victorian furnishings make Charlie's Room a favorite.

STARRETT HOUSE INN

The *Grande Dame* of Victorians

Port Townsend, on the Olympic Peninsula, is known as a "Victorian Seaport," and without doubt, one of its *grande dames* is stunning Starrett House Inn— a gem among the many fine examples of Victorian homes built in this seacoast town during the late 1800s. It and several other heritage homes have cemented Port Townsend's reputation as *the* Victorian bed and breakfast capital of Washington.

Standing in the entrance hall, your attention is drawn immediately to a breathtaking circular staircase combining Honduran and African mahogany in an alternating light and dark pattern. The stairwell culminates in a dome, with frescoes depicting the Four Seasons and Four Virtues. Each solstice and equinox, the sun shines through a red glass on the eight-sided exterior dormers, and points a beam toward the fresco representing the current season.

Left, bottom, the front parlor, showing a Schrank 1779 painted armoire from Salzburg. Below, one of the tasty breakfast dishes.

The famous spiral staircase in the Tower of Four Seasons.

Owners Edel and Bob Sokol have chosen early American antiques, which lend a certain elegance to the guest rooms. Ann's Parlor has a carved walnut bed with a romantic four-poster look, draped in a subtle floral chintz and matching quilt. From its private balcony, the room overlooks Puget Sound and the Cascade Mountains. The Drawing Room, named for the quilt and dress patterns designed there, offers three panoramic windows with a vista of Port Townsend Bay and snow-capped Mt. Baker and Mt. Ranier. Four rooms in the lower-level Carriage House have a less formal, more country feel. Brick walls, garden views, and furnishings such as wicker, a sleigh bed, or Amana Colony antiques, gives each room its own special character.

STARRETT HOUSE INN, 744 Clay Street, Port Townsend, WA 98368; (206) 385-3205. Edel and Bob Sokol, owners. Open all year. Seven guest rooms and 3 suites with water and mountain views; eight with private baths, 2 shared. Rates: $65 to $125, including full breakfast in the elegant dining room. Children over 12; no pets; no smoking; Visa/MasterCard; German spoken. Several gourmet restaurants in Pt. Townsend specialize in fish and shellfish. Kayaking, hiking, fishing, beach walks, tennis, golf, sailing, skiing, and quiet times that rest the soul.

DIRECTIONS: after leaving the ferry, turn right on Water St.; turn left on Monroe St; left on Clay St. and continue 3 blocks to the corner of Clay and Adams St.

IDAHO

PREVIOUS PAGE *and above, two views of the McCall Hotel.*

HOTEL McCALL

1930s lakeside living

Like many western towns, McCall, Idaho, boasts an altitude *higher* than its year-round population, and this logging-town-turned-resort is probably Idaho's best-kept secret. While others in the country flock to Sun Valley, Idahoans have long headed for the countryside with pine-scented forests and deep-blue waters that make McCall a trophy-fishing mecca, and mountain paradise.

PHOTOGRAPHS ON THIS AND PRECEDING PAGE BY RICKERS FILM PRODUCTIONS

In 1989, current owner Peggy Wheatcroft bought the hotel complete with its vintage furniture, which Peggy smartly re-upholstered. She hunted through antique shops, always on the lookout for the perfect 1930s touch, and the results are sprinkled throughout the inn, including a classic radio, a 1920s card table, old photos, and art deco chandeliers. Peggy even transformed the hotel's old doors into stunning painted headboards. Bridging the gap between the 1930s and the 1990s, Earl Brockman's revealing (mostly black-and-white) photographs of the area hang from many walls.

The 1990s influences become even more visible in the bedrooms, where cable television, telephones, white terrycloth robes, plumped feather pillows, and down comforters greet each guest.

HOTEL MCCALL, A Mountain Inn, 1101 North Third Street, P.O. Box 1778, McCall, ID 83638; (208) 634-8105; Peggy Wheatcroft and Chris Kirk, owners. Open all year. Twenty rooms and two suites, 16 with private baths. Rates: $55 to $90. Includes continental-plus breakfast with brewed coffee, fresh fruit, and home-baked muffins or scones. Summer Sunday brunch and weekend dinners. Wine and tea served in the dining room at 5 P.M. Children over twelve welcome; no pets; smoking on the sun deck only; American Express/MasterCard/Visa. Bike rentals, swimming, and golf nearby; skiing less than 20 minutes away.

DIRECTIONS: from Boise, take Highway 55 north. Highway 55 becomes Third Street in McCall. From Lewiston, take Highway 95 south to New Meadows, then turn east onto Highway 55 to McCall.

KNOLL HUS

A bird watcher's sanctuary

A perfect deck for bird watching.

Each spring, between February and April, more than a thousand trumpeter swans descend on the area around St. Maries, a small logging town near the western edge of the Idaho panhandle. Nine miles from town, off the main road and down a dirt lane, lies the simple, pine-paneled cottage that is Knoll Hus. Looking from its oversized windows guests can see Round Lake and the impressive birds. When the swans are not in residence, it is likely that osprey, eagles, or herons will be.

The one-bedroom, cedar-sided cabin sits like a blind on a piney hillside overlooking the lakeshore. Owner Vicki Hedlund decorated the main room simply, with crisp blue and white linens, white wicker furniture, fresh flowers, and a few nicknacks that reflect the Hedlunds' Swedish heritage. On some days Sweden seems a bit closer than usual, particularly when Vicki makes "kaaka," a puffed pancake chock-full of bacon and served with lingonberry sauce (made from berries sent by Hedlund

relatives in the homeland). On other days, guests are treated to breakfasts of ham-laced apple omelets or coddled eggs, often supplemented with piping-hot, oven-fried potatoes. Restaurants are few and far between in these woods, so Vicki will make special dinners when asked in advance.

To work off the morning meal, guests may opt to paddle the canoe, bicycle into town, or take advantage of the nine-hole golf course seven miles away. In winter, alpine skiing is less than an hour away, and cross-country skiing begins right outside the door (but bring your own cross-country ski equipment). You won't need your own equipment, however, for the working garnet mine down the road, that lets treasure-seekers screen for the purply-red semi-precious stones. The real gem is Knoll Hus itself, and its alluring solitude.

KNOLL HUS, P.O. Box 572, St. Maries, ID 83861; (208) 245-4137; Vicki and Gene Hedlund, innkeepers. Open all year except Christmas and New Year's. Reservations preferred. One-bedroom guest cottage that sleeps four; fully outfitted kitchen. Rates: $75 with full country breakfast; weekly rates from $385. Cheese and crackers for guests on arrival. Children welcome; ask in advance for current pet policy; no smoking in the cabin; MasterCard/Visa.

DIRECTIONS: from I-90, take Rte. 3 south to the marker at Mission Point. Make a right onto the dirt road and follow it for one mile. Take the first right, then left up the Knoll Hus driveway.

Left, the dining room, where breakfast is served. Above, the Executive Suite.

IDAHO HERITAGE INN

Bed and breakfast with politics

The stately looking shingle-and-clapboard house at 109 West Idaho Street saw its share of guests long before it became a bed and breakfast. First, it received visitors as the home of Governor Chase Clark; then also as the home of Clark's daughter

and son-in-law, Frank Church, U.S. Senator and presidential candidate.

Owners Tom and Phyllis Lupher adopted a political theme for their bed and breakfast inn. The Governor's Suite commemorates Chase Clark's inauguration, with a photograph of the 1940 event. The large oak bed and queen-sized mattress blend subtly with the dignified green walls and simple white curtains. Like the Governor's Suite, the Judge's Chambers boasts leaded-glass, diamond windows. Although it shares a bath with the Mayor's Study, it also shares an open-air veranda that extends across the back of the house.

In 1904, Merchant Henry Falk spent five thousand dollars to build his home, a lot of money for the time. Its water system taps into the area's geothermal resources, and the house is heated naturally with hot, mineral-rich water. Located in the historic Warm Springs district of Boise, the inn is situated only five blocks from trout fishing in the Boise River, and is near jogging and bike trails in the town's impressive greenbelt of linked parks.

THE IDAHO HERITAGE INN, 109 West Idaho Street, Boise, ID 83702; (208) 342-8066; Tom and Phyllis Lupher, owners. Open all year. Four rooms and one suite; three with private baths. Rates: $45 to $75 with expanded continental breakfast. Children welcome; no pets; American Express/MasterCard/Visa.

DIRECTIONS: from I-84, take the Broadway exit. At the end of the exit, turn left onto Idaho Street.

GREENBRIAR INN

QUICKSILVER PHOTOGRAPHY

A brick beauty

The Greenbriar stands out among its neighbors—a brick beauty tucked into a quiet residential street of predominantly wood frame homes. In fact, the Greenbriar was *meant* to call attention to itself; built in 1908 by a bricklayer, the house served as the artisan's best possible advertisement. When the McIlvennas bought the inn in 1984, they immediately set to work stripping the façade of its bright pink paint.

The former Denver stockbrokers also attacked the interior, painstakingly updating the electrical system, scraping wallpaper, and adding lovely stenciled accents in each of the nine guest rooms. After a winter's worth of renovations, the inn opened on April Fool's Day in 1985.

Surviving its tenure as a boarding house, a church, and (as legend tells) a bordello, the solid structure's finest details show up in its elegant mahogany woodwork. Besides the splendid staircase, the wood forms window seats in some bedchambers, as well as a graceful arched and columned divider that separates the bay-windowed living room from the cheerful dining room.

Guests awake to three-course gourmet meals made even more pleasant by the antique Noritake china and pleasing peach and white linens. Filling com-

binations are whipped up, such as sourbread French toast with ham-and-apple pie, or sausage-spiked cheese strata with pecan Belgian waffles. It is easy to linger here, if not at breakfast with a cup of coffee or tea, then in the evening at the outdoor hot tub.

Down comforters, which Kris McIlvenna imported from Ireland, make the beds irresistible. For special occasions, rooms number One and Six are especially light and cozy. Nestled on the third floor, these dormer rooms have all the character of garret rooms, but with unexpectedly high ceilings. Light peach and lavender set off the half-moon window, flowerboxes, and king-sized bed of number Six. No matter what the color scheme, each room unmistakably defines the purest essence of good clean comfort.

QUICKSILVER PHOTOGRAPHY

GREENBRIAR BED AND BREAKFAST INN, 315 Wallace Street, Coeur d'Alene, ID 83814; (208) 667-9660; Kris and Bob McIlvenna, owners. Open all year. Nine rooms, five with private baths, one with TV. Rates: $35 single, $50 to $69 double. Includes 3-course gourmet breakfast; dining room open to the public on weekends. Children welcome (babysitting available if given advance notice); no pets; no smoking in the house; American Express/Discover/MasterCard/Visa. Outdoor hot tub on premises. Lake Coeur d'Alene and town within 5 blocks.

DIRECTIONS: from I-90, take the Northwest Boulevard Exit to Sherman St. Turn north onto Fourth St. and go four blocks to Wallace St.; turn west. The inn is on Wallace St. between Third and Fourth streets.

The dining room, showing the magnificent corkscrew-turned dining chairs.

GREGORY'S McFARLAND HOUSE

An engaging innkeeper

Winifred Gregory may tell you she does *not* live in the past—and she doesn't. But she has some great stories to tell.

Raised in Idaho, she studied singing in New York City until, she says, impresario Rudolph Bing told her, "You're going to be a marvelous star when you're forty." The impressionable twenty-year-old turned instead to musical comedy and theater. A protégée of Mrs. Steinway, Winifred received an unusual, early American-style console Steinway piano as a wedding present.

As a guest, you might feel like a long-lost Gregory cousin. If you are visiting at Christmas, most likely you'll be included around the dinner table. Whatever time of year, the cookie jar remains filled, and coffee and tea are always at hand. Winifred does not rest until the delicious breakfasts arrive at the sunny conservatory that overlooks the rear gardens. The fare often includes New Orleans eggs or baked French toast, supplemented with Virginia ham or sausage,

Winifred's aesthetics dominate the house, and she has a definite (but not overwhelming) feminine touch. Antique four-poster beds complement the upstairs hardwood floors and Oriental scatter rugs that belonged to Winifred's mother.

GREGORY'S MCFARLAND HOUSE BED AND BREAKFAST, 601 Foster Avenue, Coeur d'Alene, ID 83814; (208) 667-1232; Winifred Howarth Gregory, owner. Open all year. Five rooms, all with private baths. Rates: $75 to $125 with full breakfast; English tea and wine in the afternoon. Well-behaved teenagers welcome; no pets; no smoking; MasterCard/Visa.

DIRECTIONS: from I-90, take the Fourth Street exit and turn right to Third Street (a one-way street going south to downtown). Watch for a Safeway parking sign and go approximately three blocks farther to Foster Ave. Turn left onto Foster and continue three blocks to Sixth Street. The house is on the northeast corner.

STEPHEN R. GREGORY PHOTOGRAPHS

STEPHEN R. GREGORY PHOTOGRAPHS

Left, top, the Rosenberry Suite; bottom, the Blackwell Suite, with spindle bed.

BLACKWELL HOUSE

From rags to riches

With a sledge hammer to knock down cubicle walls, one hundred gallons of paint stripper, 282 rolls of wallpaper, one hundred yards of border, and nineteen tons of sod, the 1904 Blackwell House has been restored to the grand old home that befits its original design.

The house was a wedding gift from wealthy lumber merchant F. A. Blackwell to his son, Russell, who became manager of the Coeur d'Alene and Spokane Electric Inter-Urban Ltd. That passenger train, consisting of three Pullmans, two day-coaches, and a sleeper, made hourly trips between the two towns.

Following years of neglect and several incarnations (including one as a halfway house for troubled youth), local businesswoman Kathleen Sims and her former innkeeper, Elizabeth Hoy, have turned this fine old house into an award-winning bed-and-breakfast inn, so beautiful in its décor and appointments that it has become a favorite location for weddings.

Names of former owners are honored on the doors of rooms and suites, which are all bright, spacious, and carefully furnished with a blend of antiques and reproductions from a sensitive, tasteful palette. Interesting pieces include a striped burgundy-brocade chesterfield with end table attached, which was salvaged from an old train, an antique rosewood grand piano, and lots of old steamer trunks serving as end tables and storage for quilts.

Omelets, huckleberry pancakes, sausages, or French toast with plum sauce are typical breakfast fare. Huckleberries, native to this area, are used whenever possible to create some of the delicacies served here.

THE BLACKWELL HOUSE, 820 Sherman Avenue, Coeur d'Alene, ID 83814; (208) 664-0656; Kathleen Sims, owner; Marge Hoy, manager. Open all year. Five guest rooms and three suites, one with fireplace; six with private baths, two sharing. Rates: $59 to 109 per room, $5 less for single person. Includes full breakfast. Children 12 and over welcome; no pets; smoking unrestricted; Visa/MasterCard/American Express. Within walking distance of 10 restaurants, from Chinese to Mexican. Downhill, cross-country, and water skiing, boating, fishing, backpacking, riding, hunting deer, elk, bear.

DIRECTIONS: *from Spokane*, take I-90 to exit 11 into Northwest Blvd. Follow to 1st St., which becomes Sherman Ave. (the main street), for 8 blocks. *From Montana*, take I-90 to exit 15 into Sherman Ave. and go 16 blocks.

BRITISH COLUMBIA

THE BEACONSFIELD

Edwardian England

When you step through the front door of this engaging inn, you are immediately transported to another time and place—an era of unadorned opulence in Edwardian England.

As a reaction to Victorian gingerbread, the Beaconsfield's exterior presents the clean and balanced Edwardian lines of buildings constructed from 1900 to World War I. Designed by gifted British Columbian architect Samuel MacLure, it has been restored to its former elegance by owner Bill McKechnie.

An airy sun room, with white and black checker-patterned floor, potted palms, wicker furniture, and peacock-feather stained-glass windows, welcomes you to the Edwardian lifestyle.

In the library on the ground floor, there is what Bill describes as the "formal 'port-and-cigar' approach to this era." Tufted leather sofas, a fireplace, book-lined walls, and luxurious carpets create the impression of an exclusive London men's club.

Each of the twelve guest rooms has a distinct

PREVIOUS PAGE: *Vancouver seen from Coal Harbor.*

appeal. Using his well-honed research skills acquired as a lawyer, Bill studied the Edwardian style carefully. He also frequented antique auctions twice weekly for two years, furnishing every room with elegant period pieces.

HUMBOLDT HOUSE

As part of Bill McKechnie's triumvirate of delightful bed-and-breakfast inns, Humboldt House is a romantic 'getaway' in an 1895 Victorian mansion. Now restored to accommodate three very special suites, each room has a fireplace, queen-sized bed, fluffy goose-down quilt, and double Jacuzzi bath.

As a guest here, you may walk the short distance to join The Beaconsfield's guests for a complimentary breakfast, or have it quietly delivered to your room by way of a breakfast door.

THE BEACONSFIELD, 998 Humboldt Street, Victoria, B.C. V8V 2Z8; (604) 384-4044; Bill McKechnie, owner. Open all year. Twelve rooms with private baths, some with jacuzzis. Rates: $100 to $196 double occupancy; children under 10 free. Full complimentary breakfast. No pets; no smoking; parking available; Visa/MasterCard.

DIRECTIONS: follow Government Street along the Inner Harbour just past the Empress Hotel; turn right on Humboldt Street; cross Douglas Street, veering right; continue 4 blocks to the inn on your left.

HUMBOLDT HOUSE, 867 Humboldt Street; (604) 384-8422. Three rooms, each with fireplace, private bath, and double jacuzzi. Booked only through The Beaconsfield. Rates: as at The Beaconsfield.

An attic suite.

OAK BAY GUEST HOUSE

An Oak Bay masterpiece

British Columbian architect Samuel MacLure was a prolific craftsman who created many elegant homes in Victoria and environs. More than one of his turn-of-the-century mansions has seen extensive renovations and been reincarnated as a bed and breakfast inn. One of MacLure's designs, the Oak Bay Guest House, was built in 1912 and as early as 1922 began its career as an inn. If rumor is to be believed, it also served briefly as a bordello!

Since innkeepers Michael Dahlgrin and Neil Boucher became owners in 1989, they have created a sense of romance in their twelve guest rooms, using eyelet bedspreads, restful pastel wallpapers and simple furnishings. Each room has an individual flavor with emphasis on quiet color schemes and lots of light. One ground floor bedsitting room is a gracious retreat with abundant windows and white walls highlighted by dark wood wainscoting and ceiling beams. The sitting area affords a cozy corner in front of the fireplace. Another features grey and white bamboo-motif walls, white wood trim, and a mini balcony decked with petunia baskets.

The second-floor sun room, which serves as the guest lounge, runs the depth of the house. It is bright, airy, and inviting, with windows on three sides overlooking the garden, wicker furniture in front of the television, and masses of flourishing indoor plants. At the other end, wingback chairs and a matching sofa provide a living-room atmosphere for enjoying the generous selection of books.

Situated close to downtown Victoria, guests can enjoy all the sightseeing pleasures of this popular city, such as high tea at the Empress Hotel, the Royal British Columbia Museum, historic Craigdarroch Castle completed in 1890, or the handsome Parliament Buildings. A short stroll away from Oak Bay Guest House is Willows Beach, one of Victoria's gems.

Ground floor suite with beamed ceiling.

OAK BAY GUEST HOUSE, 1052 Newport Avenue, Victoria, B.C. V8S 5E3; (604) 598-3812; Michael Dahlgrin and Neil Boucher, innkeepers. Open all year. Twelve rooms, 10 with private baths; 2 with private toilets and basins, shared tub. Rates: $45 to $95 single, $55 to $95 double. Full breakfast in dining room of fruit, juice, homemade muffins, and entrées such as quiche. No children; smoking in the sunroom only; no pets; off-street parking; Visa/MasterCard. Some French spoken. Good dining within walking distance or short drive away. On the city bus route.

DIRECTIONS: from downtown Victoria, take Fort Street to Oak Bay Avenue, which veers into Newport Avenue.

SUNNYMEADE HOUSE INN

An English country garden

Just fifteen minutes from Victoria, Sunnymeade House is located in a residential setting by lovely Cordova Bay. Only a few steps from the inn, a nearly-deserted beach provides marvelous opportunities to walk, enjoy a picnic, search tidal pools, or beachcomb. It is also an excellent locale for bird watchers, with tiny quail skittering over the rocks, or blue herons and sea birds foraging for food near the shore.

Owners of Sunnymeade, Jack and Nancy Thompson, are both gifted with their hands, and have combined their talents to add special touches to Sunnymeade's rooms. Jack's woodworking skills have produced sink vanities, towel racks, and ample luggage stands. Nancy has enriched the ambiance of certain rooms by designing and sewing curtains, bedspreads, lamp shades, and settee covers in English-floral fabrics.

The English country theme of Sunnymeade is also reflected in a wonderful west coast garden tended with the care that the English lavish on their gardens. Inside, the lounge, which serves also as the dining area, overlooks an attractive display of roses, petunias, geraniums, daisies, begonias, and a delicate lily pond—all made very intimate by towering evergreens.

Just around the corner is Fable Cottage, with its thatched roof and celebrated gardens. Only a short drive away, Mount Douglas Park offers a beautiful British Columbia forest with extensive hiking trails. If you drive to the summit, you will be rewarded with a magnificent 360-degree view of the city of Victoria, the Olympic Mountains of Washington State, and the Gulf and San Juan Islands.

SUNNYMEADE HOUSE INN, 1002 Fenn Avenue, Victoria, B.C. V8Y 1P3: (604) 658-1414; Jack and Nancy Thompson, owners. Open all year. Six rooms with private and shared baths. Rates: $79 to $125. Includes full country or continental breakfast. No children; no smoking; no pets; Visa/MasterCard. Dining within walking distance. Golf, tennis, horseback riding, boating, fishing close by.

DIRECTIONS: *from Victoria*: take Blanshard St. north to Hwy. 17 and continue past Elk Lake to the Cordova Bay/Sayward exit. Turn right at the light on Sayward and follow for about 4 minutes; pass Mattick's Farm and take first left, watching for B&B sign. *From ferry at Swartz Bay/Sydney*: follow Hwy. 17 south and turn left at the 7th stop light, Cordova Bay/Sayward exit. Turn left and follow directions as above from Sayward onwards.

The Rose Room.

ABIGAIL'S HOTEL

Charming and ageless

Abigail's is the inspiration of owner Bill McKechnie, who was attracted to a copy of a Rodin sculpture depicting a young woman with a flower-trimmed hat. 'Abigail' became the focus around which he developed the charming and ageless decoration of this bed and breakfast hotel.

Bill has taken great care in every detail of the luxurious interior and exterior décor. At one point during the renovation of the former 1930s apartment house, only the exterior walls remained. They still retain their classic Tudor-style character, while the trim is painted in contemporary tones of green and salmon pink. Inside, delicate stained-glass windows, crystal chandeliers, antiques, and even the plumbing fixtures were chosen meticulously. Feminine accents and delicate color combinations of peach, rose, ivory, and teal predominate in rooms named Canterbury Bell, Abbey Rose, and Foxglove.

The ground floor provides the delightfully airy reception area, a comfortable library where guests might mingle over the sherry hour, and a pleasant breakfast room. A plentiful breakfast is served from an 'open-concept' kitchen, where the chef orchestrates the meal while joining in the guests' table conversation. Eggs Abigail with smoked salmon, herb omelet, or thick French toast with whipped maple syrup, are some of the entrées which change daily.

On the top floor, four 'Celebration Rooms' offer a romantic retreat for guests who want a pampered escape from it all. With antique or canopy beds, cozy goose down quilts, fireplaces, Jacuzzis, or deep soaking tubs, guests are comfortably cocooned in carefree surroundings. There is even a private breakfast door where a food hamper can be delivered without the slightest disturbance.

ABIGAIL'S HOTEL, 906 McClure Street, Victoria, B.C. V8V 3E7; (604) 388-5363; Bill McKechnie, owner; Hazel Prin, innkeeper. Open all year. Sixteen guest rooms with private baths, some with Jacuzzis, 8 with fireplaces. Rates: $100 to $196, double occupancy. Children under 10 free. Full gourmet breakfast. No pets; no smoking; Visa/MasterCard. Located a few blocks from downtown Victoria. Specialty shopping, oceanfront walking, parks, recreation rentals, museum, theatres.

DIRECTIONS: follow Government Street along the Inner Harbour. Just past the Empress Hotel, turn right onto Humboldt Street; cross Douglas Street, veering right; continue for 4 blocks to Vancouver Street and turn left; continue 4-1/2 blocks to McClure Street; turn right onto McClure and Abigail's is at the end of the cul-de-sac.

HOLLAND HOUSE

Where art reigns supreme

Owner Lance Olsen's philosophy has produced one of Victoria's most unusual and elegant inns. "Instead of hanging paintings on empty walls and trying to sell them, I thought it would be a good idea to put beds in the rooms and rent them. We sell the art works every night, but we get to keep them, which is much better than selling them and never seeing them again!", says Lance.

Himself an artist, Lance grew up amid darkest London's Victorian buildings, and his reaction was to create rooms full of light and simplicity at Holland House. Lance and his wife, Robin, formerly an occupational therapist, have taken great care in furnishing each of the rooms with its own unique combination of antiques, locally crafted four-poster beds draped with lace, and Oriental carpets. Paintings decorate all the bedroom walls, stairways, and the lounge area. Ceramic sculptures and fine pottery adorn coffee tables and fireplace mantels. Even the chambermaid's cupboard has its own ceramic panels created by one of Lance's fellow artists.

All artwork displayed at Holland House is contemporary, representing the talents of Lance and other local artists. According to Robin, "People will find out they don't have to have modern furnishings in order to have modern art."

Located just two blocks from the inner harbor and the Seattle and Port Angeles ferry terminals, Holland House, formerly a 1934 apartment building, is at the hub of Victoria's many attractions.

All the charms of Victoria and its "Olde England" quality are within walking distance or just a short drive away. Guests at Holland House enjoy the luxury of being close to attractions which range from museums, horse-drawn carriage tours, parks, and seaside walks to specialty shopping and fine dining.

HOLLAND HOUSE, 595 Michigan Street, Victoria, B.C. V8V 1S7; (604) 384-6644; Lance Olsen and Robin Birsner, owners; Deborah Skelton, manager. Open all year. Ten rooms with private baths, TV and telephone; one ground floor room is wheelchair accessible. Rates: $100 to $175 single; $110 to $185 double. Five breakfast choices are served in the lounge or delivered to the room. Children welcome; smoking restricted to patio/balconies; no pets; Visa/MasterCard/American Express/Diner's Club; off-street parking.

DIRECTIONS: two blocks from Victoria's Inner Harbour behind the Parliament Buildings at the corner of Michigan and Government Streets.

View of the inn buildings from the herb garden.

SOOKE HARBOUR HOUSE

The crême de la crême of bed and breakfast inns

Beyond a mammoth oak tree, trimmed with hanging moss, an unpretentious white clapboard building belies the pleasures awaiting you. Nothing about the entrance to this inn prepares you for the world-class gourmet cooking and magnificently appointed rooms of Sooke Harbour House.

The 'Old House' is the hub of this celebrated inn, sitting high on a cliff encompassed by a massive herb garden and profusion of blossoms cascading towards the sea. Across the Straits of Juan de Fuca, Washington's snow-capped Olympic Mountains line the horizon. At any time of year, it's the perfect setting for a quiet getaway or romantic retreat.

Left, top, view of Juan de Fuca Strait as seen from the inn; bottom, the Victor Newman Longhouse Room, showing West Coast Indian artifacts and decorations on cedar around the bathtub and on the love seat.

Fredrica and Sinclair Philip are the energetic and accomplished hosts of Sooke Harbour House. Originally from France, Fredrica is the inn director and her gracious manner makes you feel as though you are a special guest in her home. "The feeling we want to create is one of coming back to a cottage you know", Fredrica says. Sinclair supervises the mostly-edible landscaping, goes scuba diving for seafood, and maintains a thorough knowledge of regional wines. The food is a gastronomic triumph, incorporating manifold ocean and garden treasures such as sea urchin, octopus or abalone and edible flowers or exotic herbs. Large windows overlooking Sooke Harbour circle the dining room.

Together the Philips masterminded the construction of an addition to the inn with ten highly individual guest suites supplementing three rooms in the old house. With poetic names such as the Mermaid Room, Ichthyologist's Study, and Herb Garden Room, each has its own theme and unique ambience. The magnificent Victor Newman Longhouse Room has a tasteful collection of handcrafted west coast native masks, a chieftain's bench and a carved splash panel by the tub-for-two. Every room has a fireplace, ocean view, and balcony or terrace.

SOOKE HARBOUR HOUSE, 1528 Whiffen Spit Road, R.R. 4, Sooke, B.C. V0S 1N0; (604) 642-3421; Fredrica and Sinclair Philip innkeepers. Open all year. Thirteen rooms, all with private baths. Rates: $125 to $240 double occupancy, including full breakfast, lunch, and a decanter of port by the fireplace. Dining room open to the public and guests serving internationally-acclaimed northwest cuisine prepared by youthful Canadian chefs. Stocked wet bar in certain rooms. Children welcome; pets $10 extra; smoking allowed in half the rooms; French and German spoken; Visa/MasterCard/American Express. Kayaking, hiking, sailing, windsurfing, scuba diving, tennis in the vicinity. Local cafe or pub-style dining in Sooke.

DIRECTIONS: from Victoria, follow Hwy. 1 to the Sooke-Colwwod turnoff; follow Hwy. 14 to the village of Sooke; turn left at Whiffen Spit Road, about 1 mile (1.6 km) past Sooke's only traffic light; proceed until you see the sign just before the beach.

The cedar bed in the Victor Newman Longhouse Room.

HASTINGS HOUSE

Seaside pastoral elegance

Over fifty years ago naval architect Warren Hastings and his wife moved from England to Salt Spring Island, and were immediately attracted by the seaside locale and gentle feeling of the area. They decided to build a replica of an eleventh-century manor house, similar to those they had known in Sussex.

From Mr. Hastings' drawings and designs, the post-and-beam house was built without the aid of heavy equipment, except for a tractor and concrete mixer. Hastings maintained strict control over all construction, ensuring careful attention to every detail, such as the massive Sussex-style cowled fireplace in the former living room. Special tools were designed to produce the 'adzed finish' of the rich, dark cedar beams inside what is now known as the Manor House—the focal point of today's Hastings House.

Purchased from the Hastings in 1980, the inn has been renovated and expanded to five buildings with eleven suites. In keeping with the pastoral setting at the head of Ganges Harbour, each building on the thirty-acre property provides beautifully finished suites.

Post cottage, which was originally a Hudson Bay Company trading post, is located in a fragrant garden orchard, with French doors opening off the sitting room to marvelous views of the sea. Farmhouse features two-level parlor suites, with open brick fireplaces. A walk past the croquet lawn and through sheltering woods leads to Cliffside, the most secluded accommodations, with two bedrooms, a fireplace and outside deck.

Owners Pamela and Hector de Galard spare nothing when it comes to indulging you at this

international, award-winning retreat. From individual nameplates at your door, to fresh flowers, cozy eiderdown quilts, immense bath towels, and imported soaps in your room, every comfort is carefully considered. Each morning, before breakfast, a wake-up hamper is placed by your door, with fresh juice, hot coffee, and muffins. Every afternoon you can enjoy tea served with freshly baked treats, inside the Manor House, or outside on the garden patio.

HASTINGS HOUSE, Box 1110, Ganges, Salt Spring Island, B.C. V0S 1E0: (604) 537-2362; Pamela and Hector de Galard, managers. Open from March 8 to November 30. Eleven suites, all with private baths. Rates: March 8 to May 2: $195 to $315; May 3 to November 30: $225 to $395. Gourmet breakfast and afternoon tea included. No children under 16; no pets; smoking in living room only; French, Spanish, Portuguese and German spoken; Visa/MasterCard/American Express. The dining room serves lunch and dinners. Salmon fishing, sea kayaking, boating, beachcombing, hiking, art and crafts galleries, ocean and lake swimming in the area.

DIRECTIONS: *from Vancouver Island*: veer left after leaving the ferry at Fulford Harbour and follow signs to Ganges. Go through Ganges and follow Lower Ganges Rd. taking the first major right turn (Harbour House on N/E corner); Hastings House is just beyond the marina on the right. *From Vancouver*: after leaving the ferry at Long Harbour, follow signs for Ganges, turning left immediately before town at Harbour House; continue just past the marina to Hastings House on the right. Guests without cars can be met by prior arrangement.

Left, top, full moon over Ganges Harbour on Salt Spring Island; bottom, the Post guest cottage set amidst the lush gardens.

OLD FARMHOUSE

Gourmet breakfast farmhouse style

Tucked away off one of Salt Spring Island's winding rural roads, the Old Farmhouse is a quiet enclave set amongst ancient arbutus and fir trees. Staying at this bed and breakfast is like a visit to your favorite aunt and uncle's tranquil country home.

Owners Gerti and Karl Fuss spoil you with a European flair. After years as manager of one of Vancouver's best-known restaurants and teacher of cooking courses, Gerti brings excellent skills to this delightful island refuge. Each morning, she dons a crisp eyelet apron to serve a sumptuous breakfast at a pine table in the country-style dining room.

Menus vary, but always include Gerti's delicious homebaked muffins, cinnamon buns, and croissants. Fruit is garnished with crème fraîche, and a standard entrée consists of eggs Florentine in a pastry shell with tarragon sauce and asparagus spears. Gerti

Left, top, the sitting room; bottom, a downstairs guest room. Below, the guest wing.

won't let you go to the ferry without a "doggie bag" of breakfast baked goods.

A separate entrance and terra cotta-tiled hallway lead to the four guest rooms. Using pastel hues, each room radiates a pleasing blend of delicate wallpapers, wainscoting, wicker furniture, and gleaming wood floors. The two upstairs guest rooms have vaulted ceilings with balcony French doors topped by triangular windows. Downstairs, bedroom patios open onto the spacious surrounding gardens. The property is exceptionally peaceful and you will have an undisturbed sleep in the cozy, down-comforter beds.

Karl and Gerti themselves built and decorated the guest accommodations. What they have created is testament to their vision, hard labor, and good taste.

OLD FARMHOUSE, 1077 Northend Road, R.R. 4, Ganges, Salt Spring Island, B.C. V0S 1E0; (604) 537-4113; Gerti and Karl Fuss, owners. Open all year. Four rooms, each with private bath and balcony/patio. Rates: $110. No children; no pets; no smoking; German spoken; Visa/MasterCard. Resident cats, Max and Morriz. Good dining on the island. Golf and tennis within walking distance, bicycling, fishing, riding, sailing, galleries, Saturday Farmers' Market, and June-Sept. craft show.

DIRECTIONS: *from Vancouver Island:* veer left after leaving the ferry at Fulford Harbour and follow signs to Ganges/Vesuvius. Go through Ganges and continue towards Vesuvius; pass golf course on right, then major crossroad with community hall; .3 miles (1/2 km) straight ahead, make right turn at Old Farmhouse sign. *from Vancouver:* after leaving ferry at Long Harbour, follow directions to Vesuvius; turn right at major crossroad just before Vesuvius with community hall on right; .3 miles (1/2 km) straight ahead, make a right turn at Old Farmhouse sign.

CLIFFSIDE INN

What postcards are made of

Known as the 'Island of Beaches', Pender Island is situated in British Columbia's Gulf Island archipelago, between the mainland and Vancouver Island. Its many charms make it a popular retreat. Cliffside Inn, a third-generation property, sits high above the sea—a spectacular location for observing wild winter storms or savoring summer sunsets. From the "cliffhanger" deck, postcard-like scenes extend east to Mayne Island, and south to Washington's magnificent Mt. Baker.

Local wildlife is an appealing attraction at Cliffside, and owner Penny Tomlin puts on a spectacular show for her guests when she feeds the bald eagles which swoop down gracefully onto the deck. They are only part of the rich natural environment, which also includes resident river otters and deer grazing on the lawn.

Three guest rooms face the ocean, and the fourth, facing the garden, opens onto the "cliffhanger deck." Channel View, only twelve feet from the cliff's edge, is a large combination bed sitting room with a wood-burning fireplace, queen-size brass bed, five-piece bathroom, and delicate shades of rose in the carpeting and wallpaper. The large bay window provides a striking panorama of British Columbia's natural beauty.

Channel View Honeymoon Suite with wood burning fireplace.

Left, top, the wonderful breakfast deck, which shares this view with two of the suites; bottom, the view of the outer Gulf Islands from the dining room. Below, complimentary wine is a special touch.

A delicious, full breakfast is served in the 'Cliffside Conservatory', where each table offers magnificent views. Penny's culinary skills are legendary, and her breakfast main dishes might include raspberry pancakes, Amaretto French toast, or eggs Benedict. She also bakes her own croissants, and is well known for more than twenty varieties of mouth-watering muffins.

Cliffside offers preferred rates for nearby bicycle and small boat rentals or fishing charters; and Pender Island offers wonderful walking trails and beaches to explore, or craft shops for browsing and buying.

CLIFFSIDE INN ON-THE-SEA, Armadale Road, North Pender Island, B.C. V0N 2M0; (604) 629-6691. Penny Tomlin, innkeeper. Open all year. Two rooms and two suites, each with private bath and large private patio; two with fireplaces. Private romantic hot tub sessions on Cliffhanger deck. Rates for high season: package plan of 2 nights accommodation with breakfast each morning and one 4-course gourmet dinner for two, $150 to $195 per person; single day with breakfast, $120 to $155 per couple; reduced off-season rates. 'Take Over the Inn' package, Honeymoon package, and murder mystery weekends for groups. Children over 16; pets allowed in 1 room; outside sheltered smoking; Visa/MasterCard.

DIRECTIONS: from the ferry at Otter Bay, follow signs to Hope Bay; at Hope Bay, take Clam Bay Road for 1/2 mile (.8 km); turn right at Armadale Road; 800 ft. (244 metres) to Cliffside sign on right. 2 miles (4 km) in total from ferry.

The sun deck and nature are contiguous.

FERNHILL LODGE

Historical themes

Brian Crumblehulme is a self-taught chef who came to the bed and breakfast business with his wife, Mary, after several other careers including chemistry, landscaping, and commercial herb farming. As Mary says, Fernhill Lodge is an "amalgam of our interests over the years—history, music, food".

The 18th-century French guest room.

A historical focus pervades the gardens, guest rooms and, most significantly, the gourmet dinners. House specialties include Roman, Medieval and Renaissance menus.

Breakfast is also a bountiful feast not to be underestimated, with a copious fruit dish, sundry exotic egg specialties as well as fresh muffins and scones with strawberry Amaretto jam.

Amongst towering evergreens on a secluded hill, Fernhill enjoys a tranquil five-acre setting. Five guest rooms have period themes—18th century French, Jacobean, Edwardian, Colonial and Oriental. Guests are encouraged to play a game of Medieval skittles, unwind in the sauna, or relax on the expansive sundecks with a pot of herb tea. For years, guests and food writers alike have sung the praises of Fernhill's "feast for the senses".

FERNHILL LODGE, P.O. Box 140, Mayne Island, B.C. V0N 2J0; (604) 539-2544; Brian and Mary Crumblehulme, owners. Open all year. Five rooms with period themes, all with private baths. Rates: $55 to $65 single, $80 to $120 double. Children welcome; pets by prior arrangement; smoking on decks on in sunroom in bad weather; Visa/MasterCard/Diner's Club. Mayne is noted for its cycling appeal. Sandy beaches, rural backroads, art or craft galleries, and restaurants are all within easy peddle power or by car.

DIRECTIONS: pick up a Mayne Island roadmap on the ferry. Turn left at the top of the ferry exit. Veer right, following Village Bay Road until the stop sign at Fernhill Road; turn right and continue to the Lodge sign on the right—2-1/2 miles (4 km) in total from the ferry.

GROVE HALL ESTATE

Magnificently exotic

Furnished with priceless antiques collected over many years of working and traveling in Asia and the Middle East, this bed and breakfast is a museum display. But there is nothing forbidding about the atmosphere at Grove Hall. Judy and Frank Oliver are warms hosts, encouraging guests to enjoy luxurious comfort amongst their personal treasures.

Judy's flare for decorating is evident throughout, particularly in the theme guest accommodations—the Singapore Room, Indonesian Suite, and Siamese Room. Guests in the Singapore Room can delight in an elaborately carved, teak Chinese wedding bed with gilded accents. Specially-designed Balinese batiks grace the bedspread, wall paintings and sumptuous 'papasan' rattan chair in the Indonesian Suite which also features a sitting room and balcony overlooking the lake. With its veranda over the front gardens, the Siamese Room represents a taste of Bangkok with radiant color combinations and wicker furniture. Downstairs, the living room is another mecca for antique lovers with its ancient opium bed, Chinese screen, Oriental carpets and many other priceless treasures.

Judy serves a full English breakfast in the gracious, wood-paneled dining room where the leaded glass windows provide views over the lawns towards the lake, shared by Canada geese and swans.

A long, tree-lined drive approaches the seventeen acres of property surrounding this Tudor mansion, another of architect Samuel MacLure's triumphs. A private tennis court and billiard table offer estate-style diversions for the guests.

GROVE HALL ESTATE: 6159 Lakes Road, Duncan, B.C. V9L 4J6; (604) 746-6152; Judy and Captain Frank Oliver, owners. Open all year. Three rooms with 2-1/2 shared baths. Rates: from $75 single; from $95 double. Full breakfast included. No children; smoking on porches; no pets; no credit cards; personal checks accepted. A resident dog and two cats are not allowed in guest areas. Sailing cruises and fishing at Cowichan Bay; famous outdoor wall murals at nearby Chemainus; golf courses; B.C. Forest Museum; good dining within brief driving distance.

DIRECTIONS: *from Victoria*: take Hwy. 1 north to Duncan. Cross the bridge over the Cowichan River and turn right at Trunk Road, Duncan's first set of lights. Follow Trunk Road 3/4 mile (1.2 km); turn left on Lakes Road and follow for 1 mile (1.6 km) to Grove Hall—no sign, watch for '6159'. *From Nanaimo*: take Hwy. 1 south to Duncan. Pass the B.C. Forest Museum on the left and proceed to the lights at Trunk Rd. Turn left and follow directions from Trunk Rd. turnoff as above.

Overleaf, top, Chinese opium bed; bottom, Singapore Room; right, driveway in autumn.

PINE LODGE FARM

Rustic country sophistication

Cliff and Barb Clarke have combined many years of expertise in both the restaurant and antiques business to establish their own incomparable guest house near Mill Bay on Vancouver Island. Thirty acres of land had to be cleared before they constructed their self-designed retreat, intended specifically as a bed and breakfast lodge. Rough pinewood used for both exterior and interior walls was milled on the Island. The rustic, country ambiance for this substantial home was a conscious decision, according to Cliff. "I wanted it to look old when we built it."

Inside, the main focus is an expansive and inviting two-story lounge with a commanding floor-to-ceiling fieldstone fireplace taking center stage at one end. Amidst a superb accumulation of the Clarkes' favorite antiques garnered from years of collecting and selling, guests can sink into deep cranberry-colored armchairs and read to their heart's content under a Tiffany-style lamp. Gleaming floors of cedar, fir, and hemlock wood, all cut on the property, are accented with rich Oriental and Persian carpets.

The two-story main lounge.

The picture windows frame an unobstructed view between towering arbutus (madrona) trees across Satellite Channel to the Gulf Islands. Walking trails, fields, and farm animals add to the paradise-like setting.

Pine Lodge Farm has seven guest rooms in the main building, which open off a gallery overlooking the lounge below. As with the rest of the Lodge, each room is tastefully furnished in country antiques, whether they be a white iron-and-brass bed, twin four posters, an oak armoire, or converted-to-electric period lamps. There's also a delightfully secluded cottage with two bedrooms and full kitchen—just like a private home in the country. From the cottage hot tub guests view a tranquil pond surrounded by mammoth evergreens.

The Clarkes' full country breakfast includes fruit in season, eggs fresh from Pine Lodge's own hens and served up in any number of ways, along with Canadian bacon, succulent sausage, and homemade fresh berry jams.

PINE LODGE FARM, 3191 Mutter Road, Mill Bay, B.C. V0R 2P0; (604) 743-4083; Cliff and Barb Clarke, owners. Open all year except Christmas. Seven rooms, all with ensuite showers. Cottage has 2 bedrooms, 2 baths, hot tub and fully stocked fridge for breakfast. Rates: $45 single; $65 to $75 double. Children welcome; no pets; no smoking; Visa/MasterCard; dog in residence. Good dining 10 to 15 minute drive away. Golf, sailing, fishing, swimming, boat charters, museums in the area; 40-minute drive to Victoria and short ferry ride to famous Butchart Gardens.

DIRECTIONS: *from Victoria*: follow Hwy. 1 (Trans Canada) north about 25 miles (40 km) into Mill Bay village. At the north end of the village, turn right at Kilmalu Rd. lights; turn left on Telegraph Bay Rd. and follow for 2 blocks; turn right on Meredith and go one block; turn left on Mutter and continue to end. *from Nanaimo*: follow Hwy. 1 (Trans Canada) south for about 1 hour. Turn left at the first traffic signal in Mill Bay at Kilmalu Rd. Follow directons from "turn left on Telegraph. . ." as above.

The great stone fireplace in the main lounge.

YELLOW POINT LODGE

Paradise British Columbian style

Panoramic windows in the Yellow Point's main lodge provide the essence of British Columbia's charm— the seascape. Across a broad channel, busy with yachts, fishing boats, sailboats, and tugs, evergreen-covered Gulf Islands dot the horizon. Guests may take summer cruises to isolated coves in a lovingly preserved 'cutter' boat, and enjoy picnic tea provided by the lodge. Wildlife in the area ranges from rabbits hopping across lawns to mink, eagles, seals, sea otters, and whales.

Richard Hill, the youthful owner, carries on this famed getaway's tradition, which was begun more than a half century ago by his father. Several years ago, when the main lodge was destroyed by fire, Richard and his father supervised the rebuilding process. Enormous, rough hewn timbers crown the

The main lounge showing the great stone fireplace, where guests love to congregate.

Left, bottom, the saltwater swimming pool. Below, a rustic outdoor shower set in the woods.

vast, vaulted ceiling of the sitting room, which is generously filled with comfortable sofas and armchairs. Surrounding the massive stone fireplace, with its ever-present burning logs, are other cozy seating areas which invite guests to curl up with a good book.

Accommodations range from modern to rustic. In the main lodge, some second-floor guest rooms have panoramic views of the sea. A few cottages at the water's edge are camp-style and basic; while others, nestled in the woods, are more spacious (chalet-style, with shared facilities). Further away are sheltered, private bed sitting room cottages, which also enjoy sea vistas.

Sauna, showers, and an ocean-view hot-tub huddle in a shaded grove. The two-hundred-foot saltwater pool, and secluded beaches, entice summer swimmers. Joggers and walkers can savor the wooded trails on Yellow Point's 180-acre private grounds. Tennis, canoes, rowboats, and bicycles are all available for those who are more energetic.

YELLOW POINT LODGE, R.R. 3, Ladysmith, B.C. V0R 2E0: (604) 245-7422; Richard Hill, owner. Open all year. Accommodations for approximately 100 guests in summer, 50 in winter. Lodge rates: 9 rooms, some with view, $87 to $97 single, $139 to $149 double. Barracks, cabins, and cottages range from rustic to modern with shared or private baths; rates: $47 to $97 single, $84 to $149 double. 20% discount October through April; minimum stay 2 days on weekends, 3 days on long weekends. Family style American plan meals as well as afternoon tea, morning and evening snacks; advance notice needed for special dietary needs. Outdoor professional tennis courts and all sports activities included. Children over 16; no pets; no smoking in dining room only; Visa/MasterCard. Dogs in residence, Chip and Daisy.

DIRECTIONS: *from Nanaimo*: follow Hwy. 1 south towards Ladysmith. Pass the first Yellow Point/Cedar Rd. exit; go about 1-1/2 miles (2.4 km) past Cassidy Airport, and turn left at Cedar Rd. Drive 2 miles (3.2 km); turn right on Yellow Point Road and continue 4 miles (6.4 km) to the Lodge. *from Victoria*: follow Hwy. 1 north. Pass through Ladysmith; turn right approximately 3 miles (4.8 km) north at Yellow Point and Cedar Rd. exit sign. Follow directions as above beginning "drive 2 miles. . . ". Free pickup by prior arrangement from Cassidy Airport, bus at Ladysmith, or ferry bus at Nanaimo.

Left, on the beach, with drift wood. Above, the stunning view from the breakfast table.

BEACHSIDE BED & BREAKFAST

Living on the beach

Beachside Bed and Breakfast is superbly located in West Vancouver on a quiet cul-de-sac where Gordie and Joan Gibbs are attentive hosts. Themselves adventurous world travelers, they have a reputation for taking a special interest in each of their guests.

As a former art teacher, Joan has an eye for color and design. Each guest room is delightfully decorated in soft shades of green, apricot, or blue, with an emphasis on floral linens and wicker furniture. Beautiful, fresh flowers and a fruit basket welcome each new arrival. Breakfast is served in the sun-drenched dining room, where guests can enjoy the best of Beachside's "million-dollar" view. Tasty, home-baked muffins, juice, fresh fruit salad, and delicious entrées (such as French toast and sausages) prepare guests for an enjoyable day at Vancouver's many attractions.

After a stroll beachcombing, or a day of touring, Beachside's hot tub (overlooking the sea), is the ultimate in relaxation. During the early evening, sleek, Alaska-bound cruise ships pass by, while lingering sunsets paint the sky pink, and the lights of Lions Gate Bridge and Vancouver sparkle across the sea. It is a truly glorious location, with warm, welcoming hosts.

BEACHSIDE BED AND BREAKFAST, 4208 Evergreen Avenue, West Vancouver, B.C. V7V 1H1; (604) 922-7773, Fax (604) 926-8073. Gordon and Joan Gibbs, owners. Open all year. Three guest rooms with private baths, one with kitchen, one with jacuzzi. Rates: $85 to $150, including full breakfast. No pets; no smoking; Visa/MasterCard. Hot tub overlooking the sea. Off-street parking. Resident dog, Mutley. Good city dining within easy drive and La Toque Blanche, the north shore's #1 rated gourmet restaurant, a 5-minute walk away.

DIRECTIONS: from Lions Gate Bridge, drive west along Marine Drive about 5 miles (8 km) to Ferndale. Turn left and go one half block. Turn left on Evergreen and proceed to end of cul-de-sac.

WEST END
GUEST HOUSE
Vancouver's Posh Victorian
1362 HARO ST.
681-2889

Guest room with some of the historical photographs from the house's collection.

WEST END GUEST HOUSE

Vancouver history on display

This well-loved and carefully crafted 1906 Vancouver home was built by an elderly matriarch, Melora Edwards, and ownership remained within the family for sixty years. When George Christie and partner Charles Weigum renovated it to establish a bed and breakfast, they maintained its Victorian essence along with some of its most attractive features, such as first growth cedar stair railings and door frames.

Melora's sons operated Vancouver's earliest photography business and traveled widely recording life and times in the early northwest. A fascinating collection of their historical photos portraying turn-of-the-century British Columbia is now displayed in the hallways and suites. In fact, the Edwards family presence is so strong, guests may find themselves in the company of a friendly ghost thought to be still "at home."

George and Charles have created a vision of what they themselves enjoy when traveling and have passed it on to their guests. Tea and cookies are available at the dining room buffet every afternoon. But best of all are the custom made brass beds with dream-inducing feather mattresses covered in exotic floral-trimmed linens. A nighttime sherry tray with a rose and mints adds a special touch of romance. Breakfast around the dining room table is healthy and hearty. It begins with juice, fruit plate, muffins, choice of hot and cold cereals with raisins and brown sugar, and features alternating specials such as crab, spinach, and cheddar cheese quiche or banana pecan waffles.

Located in the heart of the city, the West End Guest House is within easy walking distance of English Bay's beaches or Vancouver's famous Stanley Park, with its 1000 acres of forest, seawall pathways, gardens, and acquarium. Only one block away, Robson Street is a mecca for those in search of fine dining and fashionable boutiques.

THE WEST END GUEST HOUSE, 1362 Haro Street, Vancouver, B.C. V6E 1G2; (604) 681-2889; George Christie and Charles Weigum, owners. Seven rooms with private ensuite showers. Rates: $80 to $100, including full breakfast. Adult oriented; non-smoking; no pets; Visa/MasterCard; remote cable TV; private telephones.

DIRECTIONS: one block south of Robson Street at Broughton in Vancouver's West End.

TOR BENGTSON PHOTOGRAPHS

LABURNUM COTTAGE

Garden living

It was springtime, and the laburnum trees were in bloom with cascading yellow flowers when Delphine and Alex Masterton bought this attractive house many years ago. Instantly, they decided to call it "Laburnum Cottage", and today it is one of Vancouver's most captivating bed and breakfast inns.

Alex has turned the gardens into a wonderland that is distinctly west coast in flavor, with ferns, rhododendrons, Japanese maples, bountiful blossoms, and rock gardens—all surrounded by lofty evergreens. At one end, a brilliant-red Chinese-style footbridge leads across a creek to the self-contained Summerhouse Cottage, which evokes images of nineteenth-century garden cottages on English estates.

Each of the upstairs guest rooms in the main house has its own distinct décor, featuring delicate wallpapers, stunning antiques, and invitingly warm colors complemented by magnificent garden views.

A distinctly English flavor permeates the rooms, and the living room is no exception. Leaded windows overlook the beautiful gardens, and French doors open onto the patio. A comfortable, cushioned

Left, top, the Summerhouse Cottage, set in the back of the garden beyond the Japanese bridge; bottom, the main house, showing the garden and patio-deck.

Hosts Delphine and Alex Masterton.

window seat, rose-patterned upholstery, soft green carpet on gleaming wood floors, a fireplace, and baby grand piano make this a particularly inviting room.

Delphine's breakfasts are convivial occasions, sparked by her captivating stories and good sense of humor. From her much-loved traditional Aga grill and ovens, she produces generous helpings of delicious home-baked cinnamon rolls, muffins, croissants, and main dishes such as eggs frittata, strawberry pancakes, or shrimp and crab omelets. Breakfasting at a wrought iron table in the garden room, with its glass doors and skylight, creates the perfect atmosphere to share a leisurely beginning to the day.

LABURNUM COTTAGE, 1388 Terrace Avenue, North Vancouver, B.C. V7R 1B4; (604) 988-4877. Delphine and Alex Masterton, owner/innkeepers. Open all year. Three rooms and 2 cottages, all with private baths. Rates: $85 to $110 (Cdn.) double. No children; pets accepted; smoking outside only; Visa/MasterCard; German and French spoken. Resident cat, Geraldo. Many excellent restaurants. North shore sights include Capilano Suspension Bridge, Seymour Demonstration Park, Grouse Mt., fish hatchery, Lonsdale Quay, 9-hole golf, tennis, hiking.

DIRECTIONS: from Vancouver, follow Georgia Street through Stanley Park and across Lions Gate Bridge. Take turnoff for North Vancouver onto Marine Drive and turn left onto Capilano Rd. for 3/4 mi. (1 km.). Turn right on Paisley Ave., right on Phillip Ave. right on Woods Dr. and left on Terrace Ave. for short distance to '1388'.

Laburnum Cottage bedroom.

B & B RESERVATION AGENCIES

Oregon

NORTHWEST BED AND BREAKFAST RESERVATION SERVICE, 610 S.W. Broadway, Suite 606, Portland, OR 97205; (503) 243-7616; (800) 800-6922; LaVonne Miller, owner; Sandra Shockey, manager. 9 A.M. to 5 P.M. weekdays. Farms, ranches, Victorian, contemporary, mountain, and ocean front homes. *Coverage extends throughout the United States and Canada.*

BED & BREAKFAST RESERVATIONS—OREGON, 2321 N.E. 28th Avenue, Portland, OR 97212; (503) 287-4704; Milan Larsen. 9 A.M. to 7P.M. Monday thru Saturday. *Oregon coast turn-of-the-century architecture to ultra-modern; early 1900's to contemporary homes in Portland; ranches, farms and mountain country accommodations throughout Oregon.*

Washington

PACIFIC BED & BREAKFAST AGENCY, 701 N.W. 60th Street, Seattle, WA 98107; (206) 784-0539; Irmgard Castleberry. 9 A.M. to 5 P.M. weekdays. Mansions, Victorians, island cottages, and contemporary lakefront homes. *Covers all of Washington and British Columbia.*

TRAVELLERS' BED & BREAKFAST, P.O. Box 492, Mercer Island, WA 98040; (206) 232-2345; Jean Knight. 8:30 A.M. to 4:30 P.M. weekdays. Guest houses, inns, and private residences. *Over 200 accommodations in the Pacific Northwest, including Vancouver and Victoria, British Columbia. Assists in personal itineraries including ferries.*

Idaho

BED & BREAKFAST OF IDAHO, 109 West Idaho Street, Boise, ID 83702; (208) 342-8066; Tom and Phyllis Lupher. Furnishes information on the thirty bed & breakfasts in Idaho; makes reservations for selected places. 7 A.M. to 11 P.M. seven days a week. *Includes everything from ranch and farm stays to city bed & breakfasts.* Credit cards accepted by some.

British Columbia

AAA HOME AWAY FROM HOME BED AND BREAKFAST, 1441 Howard Avenue, Vancouver, B.C., V5B 3S2, Canada; (604) 294-1760, Fax (604) 294-0799; David and Irene Myles. Personalized accommodations from single to king beds in private homes. Private or shared baths, hearty breakfast included. MasterCard, Visa, weekly rates. *Covering Vancouver, Victoria, and Whistler.*

AA ACCOMMODATIONS WEST BED AND BREAKFAST RESERVATION SERVICE, 660 Jones Terrace, Victoria, B.C. V8Z 2L7, Canada; (604) 479-1986. Single, double, and twin rooms, with shared and private baths and full breakfast. Many accept children and small pets. Assistance with itineraries. No fee for service, major credit cards. *Covering Victoria, Gulf Islands, and up-island locations.*

ALL SEASON BED AND BREAKFAST AGENCY, Box 5511, Station B, Victoria, B.C. V8R 6S4, Canada; (604) 595-2337; Kate Catterill. A personal reservation service in heritage and residential homes, cottages, farms, and private suites. Breakfast included, small pets allowed in some. Brochure and sample listing available. Visa, MasterCard. *Vancouver Island and the Gulf Islands.*

BEST CANADIAN BED & BREAKFAST NETWORK RESERVATIONS, 1090 West King Edward Avenue, Vancouver, B.C. V6H 1Z4, Canada; (604) 738-7207; Robert and Jane Oudenaarden. Office hours from 9 A.M. to 9 P.M. seven days a week. Bed & Breakfast in the British tradition with homeowners living on premises. From luxurious to traditional accommodations with full breakfast included in from one to four rooms. *Country and city accommodations in British Columbia and Western Alberta, Edmonton, and Banff.*

BORN FREE, 4390 Frances Street, Vancouver, B.C. V5C 2R3, Canada; (604) 298-8815; Norma McCurrach. Accommodations include luxurious homes with swimming pools, saunas, English gardens, good breakfasts, and hospitable hosts. *Vancouver, Victoria, Whistler, and other areas throughout British Columbia.* (Ms. McCurrach is founder of the B.C. Bed & Breakfast Association.)

CITY & SEA BED & BREAKFAST AGENCY, Box 421, Station E, Victoria, B.C. V8W 2N8, Canada; (604) 385-1962; Pat Gordon. A group of homes offering double, twin, and queen beds, some with ensuite baths, some with self-contained suites, all with full breakfast. All homes conform to standards set by the American Bed & Breakfast Association.

GARDEN CITY BED & BREAKFAST RESERVATION SERVICE, 660 Jones Terrace, Victoria, B.C. V8Z 2L7, Canada; (604) 479-9999; (604) 479-1986; Doreen Wensley. Offering single, twin bedded, and double rooms with shared and private baths, with full breakfast included. Many accept children and pets. Major credit cards accepted, no fee for service. *Covering Victoria, Gulf Islands, and up-island locations.*

HOSTS OF THE SOUTH WEST COAST BED & BREAKFAST VANCOUVER ISLAND, 7954 West Coast Road, R.R. #4, Sooke, B.C. VOS 1N0, Canada; (604) 642-6534; Betty Morton. Association of sixteen bed & breakfasts in Sooke, 50 km (30 mi) west of Victoria. Offering single to king beds with rural to waterfront panoramic ocean views. Includes a small hotel, homes (some with suites), cottages, and farms. Some wheelchair accessible. Credit cards accepted by some members.

OLD ENGLISH BED AND BREAKFAST REGISTRY, Box 86818, North Vancouver, B.C. V7L 8L6, Canada; (604) 986-5069; Vicki Tyndell. Offering double and queen beds and full Canadian breakfast. Suites with private and shared baths, fireplaces, and pools available. *Covering Greater Vancouver. North and West Vancouver.* Visa, MasterCard.